CONFESSIONS OF A COMPASSIONATE FELON

Confessions of a Compassionate Felon

A COLLECTION OF CONVICTIONS,
CONTEMPLATIONS

&

POETIC PERSPECTIVES

BY

b.anthony.shepperd

PALMETTO
PUBLISHING
Charleston, SC
www.PalmettoPublishing.com

Copyright © 2024 by b.anthony.shepperd
All rights reserved

No portion of this book may be reproduced, stored in a retrieval system, or transmitted in any form by any means–electronic, mechanical, photocopy, recording, or other–except for brief quotations in printed reviews, without prior permission of the author.

Paperback ISBN: **9798822966383**

Contents

Confession of a Compassionate Felon	1
Who Am I…?	3
THE MONSTER WITHIN	4
THE CONSEQUENCES OF GANG MEMBERSHIP	8
METAMORPHIC	14
As This Man Thinks	18
Inga	21
Farewell To Yesterday (my suicide note)	25
If It Wasn't For Prison…	29
Am I Invisible?	31
A View Outside The Window	35
The Diamond	37
When (Colored) Boys Become Men <the prelude>	38
When Boys Become Men	39
Confession of a Compassionate Felon #2	43
My Light	46
A Fotograf 1980	49
I Was Raised By…	50
Thoughts Off The Top Of My Head	52
STIGMA	54
The Other Side of Life	55
AN UNNECESSARY LIFE	58
I Don't Know, Jus' Thinkin'…	63
Eau de Skidrow	65
An Effort For Heaven	67
Justa Letchu Know	73
Postmark From Paris	75
Girl On The #7 Bus	83
A Convo About Crutches	85
I Wonder…	87

#BeautifullyTorn	89
#flashbang!	91
#Isolated Chaos	92
Look, Just Listen… (A Love Letter)	94
The Juggler	97
Who U Talkin' To?	99
Truly	100
A Necessary Tragedy	101
The Dark Side of Truth	108
A Fotograf 2020	113
What I See in The Tenderloin	114
The Peoples' Liaison (Just An Idea)	115
3hree After 3hirty	119
Suffocation	121
In No Sense	122
Jus' Cauz	123
Less Than Zero	124
U Mist Me, Really?	125
Auditions	126
Butterflies & Hummingbirds	127
Irony, or Hypocrisy…?	128
Huh?	129
Futile	130

Confession of a Compassionate Felon

There's a lot that can go wrong when you're not afraid to die. I was fourteen when I witnessed my first murder. I saw the rival's eyes narrow into sinister slits only nanoseconds before they reversed course and bucked as wide as beverage coasters. Shock and fright and flight all traffic jammed in his brain circuitry, rendering him petrified in place.

I saw the freaky excitement register across the driver of the stolen Toyota Tercel, the auto that had been grand-thefted for the very occasion to slaughter an adversary. The driver all but wiped away a thread of drool in great anticipation of the thunderous blast that would snatch the breath of Boy Blue.

I saw the uncalloused hands roll down the passenger-side window, pull up the sports themed bandana over the bridge of his nose, shielding his innocence and his misanthropic treachery. I saw when the delinquent juvenile made eye contact with his cornered quarry, when he didn't squint, when he clutched the twin triggers of the double-barrelled sawed-off shotgun like a 1920's mobster, when his thoughts preceded the action that set off the explosion of double-ought buckshot into the neck and chest of somebody's beloved son. Father. Brother. Neighbor.

I saw when the unnamed body collapsed on the gritty, nasty, graffiti-tattoo'd sidewalk. I saw when the body jerked, as soul and spirit freed themselves from their body suit. I saw through my peripheral view, even before I heard the screams and shouts and threats and cuss words, the onlookers and bystanders ran for cover, ducking like insurgents hearing the too-late thrumble of an F16 interrupting the sound barrier.

I saw the applause and adoration and approval written across the faces of my elder peers when we returned to the safety and sanctity of our block, our turf, our red and black checked side of the chessboard.

I felt the validation of peer acceptance, the much sought cradle of "Family" relevancy, with every fist pound, and handshake I exchanged with the veterans and villains of my gang hierarchy.

There's a lot that can go wrong when you aren't afraid to die.

Writer's Insight

1989. 14 years old. My introduction to an anti-lifestyle that no juvenile delinquent should be offered membership into. I graduated early from writing on walls and fighting, to hunting for rivals with semi-automatic weapons and contemplating the number of attendants at my funeral, all of which manifested before I was old enough to attend prom. Well, except my early funeral. Instead of death, I accomplished Life in prison, which, ironically, is a much slower form of death by a thousand tiny slices.

A lot can go wrong when you aren't afraid to die.

So much more can go successfully when you aren't afraid to fail.

Who Am I...?

I took a life before I made a life
I fought life before I caught life
It was on me way before it was in me
I let it begin me...but, I won't (wouldn't) let it end me

THE MONSTER WITHIN

I often have discussions with my homeboys and close komrades, and the misguided youngsters that I'm around, about being true to who they are. I mean, who they ***really*** are.

As loyal participants in the criminal lifestyle, i.e., Gangstas, Hustlers, Players, Pimps, etc., we get so caught up in the labels that we attach to ourselves, and the images that we create, we forget who we are inside. We lose sight of the values and principles we were raised with. Our nicknames and monikers, whether we earn them or give them to ourselves, serve as a sort of avatar that we not only hide behind, but we come to find comfort and security in.

When we are initiated into the gang, and the lifestyle it encompasses, we affix a new name to the "being" that we will from then on be known as. We may be born, "John Smith", but as newly christened gangbangers, we become "Crazy Boy", "Diablo", "Killer", or whichever name may be chosen.

As we indulge in daily activities - the lawlessness and chaos we invite - we feed our insatiable egos and build upon that name with fame (infamy) and notoriety, the fuel of attention that we crave. Any principles of morality we may have learned from our parents as "John Smith", is negated, as "Killer" is fed from the trough of peer acceptance and approval, fraternal respect, and attention from the opposite sex.

In a lot of ways, the contrast between our authentic self and our created self is similar to the story of *Frankenstein*. We create an alter-ego, our "monster" of sorts, that we get so lost in the awe of, that not only do we lose control of it, but the monster can, and usually does, end up destroying us.

In the case of the monster created by the scientist, Dr. Frankenstein, the doctor, disheartened and disgusted by his own personal inadequacies and insecurities, wanted to create the "perfect man". His intention was to use the very best of everything, that is, the strongest legs and the most capable hands, the heart of the most charitable person, the brain of the intellectually prodigious. Though his intentions were truly altruistic, it was the folly of his trusted assistant that altered his plan. While retrieving from the doctor's laboratory the brain of choice, the assistant dropped it, thus destroying it. For fear of reprisal from the doctor, the assistant grabbed the very next container that held a brain and brought it to the doctor. This brain was from a certified lunatic. Unbeknownst to Dr. Frankenstein, he inserted the brain and reanimated his "perfect man". Much to his dismay, he had created a monster that he could not control, and ultimately died by the hands of.

The monster that Dr. Frankenstein had **created**, had given life to, killed him.

When we create our alter ego, our "Killer", we get caught up in the attention that is subscribed to it. Now, when we do our dirt for the sake of the gang, to uphold the vows we took, it's "Killer" who receives the praise. With each brash adventure our notoriety increases. Our egos are ecstatic! Soon, we cease to identify with who we were, "John Smith", and only wish to be acknowledged as our alter ego, our avatar, our monster. As we go through our trials and tribulations, our activities and agitations, it's our monster that receives the adulation. The monster has now taken over our authentic self.

We've lost. The person we were, and the monster that we are now, are as mutually exclusive as night and November. It's only if we are fortunate to live long enough to mature, that our authentic self can have hope. If we can reconcile who we were - the person we were created to be - with the knowledge of right and wrong, only then can we destroy the monster.

Unfortunately, we often get chopped down in our prime. Whether it's death in the streets or life in prison, we rarely get the opportunity to take back what is ours to reclaim: **ourselves**! It's much more difficult to destroy the monster than it was to create it. If left alone, "Killer" can forever alter "John Smith's" progress. Even if "John Smith" can eventually destroy the avatar of "Killer", the imprint that is left behind is far too indelible to completely fade away.

To kill the monster within we must first be willing to confront the issues that compel us to rebel on our authentic self in the first place. In order to destroy the monster, we must destroy the **need** for the monster.

February 7, 2012

Writer's Insight

2012 was a year of personal realization and revolution for me. I was confronted by the futility of my then current condition (serving a life term, still actively affiliated, progressing politically = **realization**) and the growing desire to change (wanting to be free from prison someday, needing to be a son for my mother whose memory was losing patience, wanting to be a husband and a leader for my family, needing to progress and prosper for the betterment of the underserved, called to be a beacon of light for those still staggering in the dark = **revolution**).

This cathartic confrontation evoked within me a lot of jekyll and hyde-like inner dialogue.

The Monster Within is the result of that inner discourse.

THE CONSEQUENCES OF GANG MEMBERSHIP

One of the worst feelings in the world, one of the ugliest, nastiest, most disgusting feelings in all the world, is the first morning you wake up in jail. The reality of what you've done sets in, the impossible uncertainty of what may happen - what will likely happen - weighs on you like a ton of deadly sins.

I woke up early in the morning, so early, it was still dark outside. I use the term "woke up" lightly, because I never really slept for more than a few moments at a time. I felt a strange mixture of fear, anxiety, stress, and doom - all feelings I'd experienced before, but never all at the same time.

The loosely-tied, ultra-thin bedsheets slid noisily against the course, unyielding plastic-covered mattress that was too thin, too loud, and too much of a million other things! The cell was unnecessarily quiet. It was cool, with a vent that didn't blow out a blessing or suck away my misery. Still, my unease and anticipation of everything and nothing, had me shivering like a puppy with parvo.

I was in Eastlake Juvenile Hall. Again.

I had been through these halls and units, in and out of "the box" so many times, that the staff and counselors didn't ask my name anymore. They'd just shake their heads at me like, "Damn, you just can't stay out!"

Juvenile hall was a rite of passage for a young, active gangbanger as I had been. So laying there in the one-size-fits-all-but-can't-quite-fit-me boxers and much too tight t'shirt, I trembled with a dreadful sense of…what was it? Fear?

Anguish?

Panic?

It was the worst feeling I'd ever felt. I had been charged with a murder. I did it. The detectives knew I did it, and my future was not looking good. My young mind created images that I had never considered before: prison.

Life in prison.

DEATH in prison!

I wasn't even convicted yet. But already, in my mind and in my heart, I was condemned.

It's the worst feeling in the world.

It took three years. I fought hard and I fought long, but in the end I lost. Convicted in trial and sentenced to a million years. Actually, it was 46-to-life, but it might as well have been a million years.

I was nineteen when I stood before the judge and received my sentence.

Now I was on my way to prison to serve an eternity.

Forever. For *ever*. .

I somehow convinced myself long ago, probably while I was still in the halls, that this was my fate. I had taken a VOW to "Ride and Die" for the turf.

For the 'Hood, the Homies, the Set. For the notoriety and for the infamy. I gave my oath of service for it all. And for death before dishonor, I would give my all.

But damn! Life in prison is a long time! I had only been alive 19 years! With a 46-to-life sentence, I was expected to serve at least 46 years before I could be considered for parole!

Hold up…!

You mean, a life-sentence means that after 46 years, I will only be considered for release?

As in, *MAYBE*?!

The Homies didn't tell me that! When I was getting put-on and pledging my vow of undying loyalty, nobody said anything about living in a small, cold, concrete-and-steel box, with only a slit for a window that has been painted over from the outside so you can't really see outside (whose bright idea was that?!), that gets too hot in the summer, and can't-quite-breathe hot in the really scorching months, forever, with a *possibility* of *maybe* getting out after 46 years!

DAMN!

So, after ten years of riots and stabbings and acting a fool.

Ten years of sitting in The Hole (Solitary Confinement/Ad-Seg) for 10 months, 16 months, 6 months, 11 months, 10 months..

Ten years of "Returned To Sender" letters from the same homeboys I'd grown up with, put in work with, made promises to and received promises from.

Ten years of, "Dear Mama, I need…"

After ten years of all of that, and more, I still hadn't learned anything. I mean, I'd earned my G.E.D. I had read more books than I had ever seen when I was free. I was teaching and schooling the young homeboys who would trickle through, who were hitting the yard "young, dumb, and full of gunpowder", just as I had been; how to survive in a maximum security prison, instead of training them properly about how to stay out of one. Sure, I had learned something.

But I was still banging. I was still sacrificing myself for the loyalty to, and the recognition of, the gang, the turf and the homies. I still cared more about what they thought about me and my activities in prison, than they, in reality, actually cared.

What's worse, I still cared less about what my Mom, my Father, and what my Son thought (yeah, I left a baby boy, MY baby boy, out there, while I was selfishly and carelessly pursuing death, or, more appropriately, LIFE in prison).

The saddest part of it all was that as much as I wanted to go home, as much as I wanted to be free, I wasn't ready.

-

What about me had changed? How would I have been better than I was when I came in?

How could I possibly have contributed positively and pro-socially to society?

To my community?

To my family?

To my Son?

So, ten more calendars went by. I was now thirty-six years old.

My Son was twenty-one.

And he had become a father of a beautiful little girl.

My Grand-Daughter. I was a grandfather.

And I was still banging!

But I was still banging, because honestly, after 20 years in prison, 24 years of membership I didn't know anything else. My identity and personality and pride were all as one with my gang. I was my Gang and my Gang was me. I couldn't walk away from it because I hadn't gathered the courage to admit that I didn't need the gang. I didn't know who I was without the gang. At that point in my life, I had been gangbanging and had been in captivity longer than the time I had lived free. My fear of being alone, of being an individual, kept me a prisoner of my own affiliation.

In my 21st year, I just got tired of it all: the artificial love, the superficial loyalty, the whole plastic-ness of gang politics. I was done.

I began to question what my participation meant to the cause of gangbanging, the association and affiliation of pack activity? In the grand scheme of things what had it ever meant? No matter what I did as a "Ridah" for the turf, it didn't translate into anything worthwhile to those who meant the most to me.

It offered nothing of substance to my life. My Mother was getting older. My Dad had died a few years earlier..

Yeah, my Dad died wanting to see his son free and living happily as the man he'd always wanted me to be. As God had designed me to be.

The homies didn't tell me about any of this when I was getting put-on 25 years earlier. No one had informed us at the gatherings and functions that I'd sit behind bullet-scarred, gray walls, watching those who really love me grow old and older and older, then die slowly.

No last hugs and kisses. No final goodbyes.

When my Dad died, all I received was a phone call, surrounded by six faceless correctional officers. Listening to my Mom cry, explaining that my Dad, the only Dad I would have, passed away the night before.

The homies didn't tell me that I wouldn't be able to hold my Mom while she cried.

The homies failed to tell me a whole lot.

Now, at the time of this writing, I've been in prison for 23 years.

I retired from gangbanging and all affiliations with it, from crime, and from any association with anything that will keep me away from a positive consideration of freedom. I now actively speak with prisoners, encouraging them to give up the gang mentality. That's really what it is in my opinion: a mentality. We become the person or thing that we convince ourselves that we are.

We tell ourselves that we're Soldiers and Warriors and "Ridahs" and that's who we become.

And that's exactly what it takes to walk away from it all. More importantly, that's what it takes to never walk into it in the first place.

You have to understand, to believe, that your life is far more precious, far too important, to be just another name on a wall. Life decisions (especially, Life-sentence carrying decisions) can't be made before you've even begun to live your life.

Believe me I learned that the hard way.

I've been climbing this mountain for 23 years now, only halfway to the "Maybe".

I also learned something else. The worst feeling in the world, the ugliest, nastiest, most disgusting feeling in all the world, is not the first morning that you wake up in jail.

The worst feeling in the world is receiving a phone call from someone saying that your child, your loved one, the one person that you adore more than anything on this planet has been murdered senselessly by a gangbanger for no excusable reason.

Nothing compares to that.

That's the feeling I gave to the family and loved ones of my victims.

I just wish that it hadn't taken me so many years to understand that.

METAMORPHIC

Who (or, what?) gives the caterpillar the audacity to want to change? The absolute courage to become something so different from itself - a butterfly- that it no longer contains any semblance of what it once was…of what it was born to be.

Or maybe that's just it. Maybe it was born to become something else…

Aren't we all?

Isn't life all about change? Progress? Metamorphosis?

I mean, the caterpillar emerges from its egg a small, fuzzy squirmy thing with ninety-something sticky little feet, and it just rejoices in the fact that it is what it was born to be…

A caterpillar.

…But not yet what it's meant to become.

So it feeds itself and it feeds and feeds and it travels from tree to tree to branch to leaf, just feeding. It's not concerned with fitting in or hiding, or…acceptance.

It just feeds itself.

It's preparing itself for what it's to become. It has to consume enough to sustain itself for the journey to the next phase of its life.

At some point it stops…as if to contemplate. It's had its fill and it's satisfied. Its transformation is inevitable. The caterpillar has reached a point in its development where progress is undeniable.

He's changing…evolving…becoming…

What for a time was a fuzzy caterpillar, will emerge from its chrysalis, from the safety and security of its cocoon, as a beautiful and majestic butterfly. The symbol of all that is light and peaceful and amazing.

The essence of freedom.

It will fly and find fellowship with thousands of millions of other butterflies who've just accomplished the same transformation.

And not one will ever question why any of the others changed…

…why any other didn't want to remain repressed and unevolved…
…why it was trying to better itself and flutter among the similarly audacious…

None will ever question its loyalty or commitment to one cause or another.

Because change is life…
…Life is evolution…
…Evolution is metamorphic.

Nothing remains as it is.

No one and no-thing is strong enough to defy nature, though we may try. We claim to be who we are 'til our very last breath, but it's impossible.
And foolish.

We should **strive** for change. To **evolve**. To become the very best that is in us to be…whatever that is.

We've crawled along the ground, being the least we can be for too long, just getting by, being "good enough", most of us knowing the potential that thrives within us, desperately threatening to emerge, refusing to be restrained any longer.

Yet, we stifle it. We snuff it out and ignore and deny our own eminence.

It is in us all to be greater than we are *right now*.

We have to stop fighting against ourselves, against what is natural, and embrace the change.

Be greater than you are now.

> "Be not conformed to the world, but be transformed by the renewing of your mind…"
> Romans 12:2

28 July 2012

Writer's Insight

I wrote this at a time when I had made the biggest decision in my life at that time. I had recently announced my retirement from gang banging, had denounced all association with the affiliation that I had known for far longer than I hadn't. I was unstable in my walk as a civilian, not really knowing what that would look like.

Honestly, I was second-guessing my decision. I had so much self-doubt about my inner strength and about my "testicular fortitude" to proceed.

I wrote this piece about the caterpillar and butterfly, because I had to *see* and *hear* my inner argument, just to comprehend the evidence that I am **created** to rise above the bedlam, to flutter and flow with the evolved. To inspire change. To lead by example. I fed and fed on the leaves of every book that I found, then I wrote and spoke and walked in my truth.

Then I rose above it all…metamorphic.

As This Man Thinks

"As a man thinks in his heart, so is he…", this is the wisdom of God as translated through King Solomon. Wisdom is eternal. It is relatable three thousand years after the fact, after it was first spoken or written; after it's countless translations and interpretations. As i think or believe in my heart, so i will be.

Some years ago, while i was in a prison cell with an older homeboy - a wise, but, foolish, village griot - he told me something that i'll likely never forget. It's a verse of wisdom that i have shared with many, that i have taught with for a few. He told me: "That which can be thought about, can be brought about." In essence, we are the power behind our own thoughts. We give energy to the very notions that we entertain. Our minds are the greatest computers that have ever been, will ever be, created. Our convictions are merely the arithmetic of our souls - individually, yet, collectively - manifested from our gravest desires, insecurities, and intellectual calculations. As a person, and, as a people, we can only advance to the extent that we feed our thoughts.

The other maxim that i learned some years ago, something somewhat similar to the Biblical Proverb, "As a man thinks…", is a quote from famed author, Kurt Vonnegut: "We are who we pretend to be, so we must be careful about who we pretend to be."

I was introduced to this jewel in 2007, while sitting in Tehachapi State Prison's Ad-Seg, fighting a prison gang validation. I took those words, and allowed each syllable to ping-pong around in my brain, giving space for the subtle warning to confront my then-current situation. On one hand, i vehemently denied and denounced any affiliation or association with the prison gang, even if my heart pounded for Black people empowerment, pro-Black politics, and urban community unification. On the other hand, I still breathed street gang terrorism; i condoned, promoted, and instigated Black-on-Black crime. My very own racist double-standards undercut any designs that i might have contributed to Black and Brown community unification.

So i had to ask myself: which of my staunch ideologies was merely a pretense? Who was i pretending to be? Truth is, i was, and i still am, a people person. The difference being…i now promote, and practice, spiritual, emotional, and physical health and positivity.

"Man is buffeted by circumstances so long as he believes himself to be the creature of outside conditions, but when he realizes that he is a creative power…he then becomes the rightful master of himself…" (As a Man Thinketh, by James Allen)

When we become Master and Commander of our thinking, we then will be capable of navigating ourselves through, and beyond, the circumstances that surround us.

Written: Sept. 9th, 2019

Writer's Insight

I wrote this essay as homework for an assignment that was issued out to a group of participants, a men's self-help group, called "Boys 2 Men". In this group the "older" men, about 4 of us, mentored the younger generation of men, all of which were 20-somethings, all of which had a chip on their shoulders, for one perceived injustice or another.

Solutions are often sought, but truly, how many are actually applied as remedies to the problems that instigated the discussion for solution-seeking in the first place? "Boys 2 Men" was a mentorship that walked the walk, priding itself on accountability and self-actualization.

Many lives were transformed, several trajectories were altered course for the better. The vision of a better lifestyle was fostered, imaginations were nurtured, thoughts came to life…from Boys to Men.

Inga

I fell in love with her when I was twelve.

Although I'd known her all my life, it wasn't until my prepubescent eyes saw her that I began to WANT her, to be a part of her. She was older than me by several years, but she didn't care. And, most assuredly, I didn't give a damn. I wanted her. So, at twelve years young, I began to claim her as mine. I knew she had a history. I knew she had several other boys, and even men, who had fallen for her. I didn't care. I knew she'd been around the block so many times that she had actually become synonymous with it.

I didn't care.

*I wanted Inga in my life. I wanted her to **BE** my life. I wanted Inga so bad, that I felt like I **NEEDED** her. And right there, at twelve years early, I knew that I would do and defy and disobey everything, and anyone, to have her.*

And, I got her.

Although I was only "claiming" her as mine, we didn't actually consummate our relationship until I was fourteen. That's when my lust for Inga became love. My airy daydreams and fantastic fantasies had become reality. I was in love! I was her lover and she mine. I would fight to defend her, pledge my very last breath to our bond, and vow to her my undying fidelity.

She was my girl…

NO!

*Inga was my **WOMAN**. And for years I was faithful. She, in turn, was faithful to me. I mean, she was linked to other men,* and boys, and, quite a few girls, but our love was unique. Ours was special. And, I represented our love -displayed it- with my tattoo'd heart, as others displayed their wedding rings. Because, in actuality, in all truth and circumstance, we were married. In my mind, heart, and spirit, Inga and I had been married since the summer I turned fourteen. The same summer that she made me a man. Even when I fell to a lengthy prison sentence two years later, she was there with me. And, if it was even possible, our love grew stronger. As I matured, so did our bond. I grew into manhood, and Inga guided me along, always there, always by my side, hand in hand.

My girl. My woman.
My wife.
Then, at some point, I really don't remember when exactly, but things changed. Something, or, some things, just changed. It wasn't the love or the bond, it was...something. But, of course I ignored it. I chose to not confront it, with hopes that it was nothing. Our love was solid, I often convinced myself. Six or seven or ten years into my life sentence, my heart still beat fast for Inga. She was still always wherever and whenever I needed her.

My woman. My wife.
My bitch. Yeah, my **BITCH!** Because, somehow, somewhere, Inga started acting strange. She was no longer there for me when I called. I mean, I had known that she had other men, other relationships, entertained other interests. But, I had thought, **believed,** that what we shared was special. It was precious and supposed to be forever and ever and ever. Remember our vows? Or, at least, my vows to her? And, my pledges! Surely, she would remember those… Well, at the very least, remember my tattoo'd heart. I had done it all for her. For Inga.

I mean...I had known she was a free spirit, untamed, and feral as young love. But, I never thought she'd become a **WHORE!**
Never! Not ever!
I was getting letters from my closest homeboys who had first-hand accounts of how Inga wasn't Inga anymore. She was barely even a shadow of her former self. And definitely, most assuredly, she was not the girl that I had fallen in love with.
"Its all bad, homie!", one friend would say.
*"Its **ugly**, dawg!", another would tell me.*
But, I didn't hear it. Well, I heard it, but I didn't listen. Inga was mine, and I was hers. Till Death Do Us Part, and all that. If anyone could bring her back from this insanity and return her to her principles, it would be me. And I tried. I tried...
And, I tried.
Inga changed, and became worse. But, I stayed with her. Not for the remnants of love that was now unrequited. Because, truthfully and sincerely, the Me that I am now understands that the love was never requited. But, I stayed with her. Twenty five years, it's been. Because, I had never been without her. I had never walked without Inga beside me. Our love was...symbiotic.
In truth, I was who I was - gangsta, souljah, criminal, comrade, monster - because, Inga had instilled in me a false sense of bravado and chauvinism, something that my young, impressionable psyche wasn't ready for. She'd given me everything I'd wanted...or, thought I'd wanted. Inga had provided my costumed-disguise of confidence and arrogance, things that I wore well. She told me to live my life unashamed and unapologetic.
Now she's dying.
Although she may never die completely, she is definitely dying. In my heart.

As un-gentlemanly, and as un-chivalrous, as it may be to do, I'll divorce from her, as she stands before me, ever-present, wheezing and coughing, dying, and dying, and dying.

Because, to me, the love is already dead.

The End

Written: sometime/someday/2012

Writer's Insight

"Inga" is my ode to lost love. Gang banging is/was the greatest love of my life. So much so, that I reminisce about the best of the puppy love stage, the tumultuous moments that threatened to destroy me, and the latter times when it was nearly impossible to make a clean break. I vowed a marriage of "Til my very last breath do us part", and in a lot of ways, it was just that.

Inglewood, California…I loved her, I miss her, forever & beyond…

Farewell To Yesterday (my suicide note)

I hope it ends as abruptly and as unpremeditated as it began twenty-something years ago...

The finality of it all, even if at first only subconsciously, is comforting. Achieving the all-encompassing solace that I'd never-ever considered possible in this populace of paparazzi and "ah-ha gotcha! gossip", that invades and permeates every crevice, every minute fissure of my physical and emotional being, lost and tucked away forever in prison.

No longer will I be the caged beast, poked and teased, scourged and taunted.

No longer will I be the indentured servant to a debased, immoral, vicious miscreant master.

No longer will i be...

My farewell from this life, from this suspended existence, from this savage planet, is momentary...

To those who love me, those who know me – REALLY know me – forgive me. What began as a transitory lapse in judgment, manifested to become a two-and-a-half-decades long excursion from the frying pan to the fire, seering away all but the core of who I am. Painfully, I have come to realize that i'm not as strong as i'd once believed. This life, i'll reluctantly admit, is no longer worth living.

To those who **thought** they knew me, wanted to know me, who created their own idolatrous versions; those whose

CONFESSIONS OF A COMPASSIONATE FELON • 25

secrets i kept to the extent that my psychological matrix suffered beneath the burden of inverted honor — like a child resigned to the punishment of holding volumes of encyclopedias with outstretched limbs, resisting, with utter futility, to give in to gravity and reason — i crumbled. I've broken into a million shards, shattered, and you stepped over me like something you'd prefer not to have to scrape off your shoe later. And still, i remain fractured, unglued, motionless — and no one, not one of you, offered even to sweep me into a dustpan and toss me into the wind, to be scattered afar, further forgotten…

To those who wanted to know me, i apologize posthumously. For as surely as you read these words, my words, i'm now long gone from this world, this cell, this…penitent-iary.

I would have liked to have known you, i'm sure, because, contrary to popular belief, i am friendly. I possess an uncanny talent for putting your fears, worries, shortcomings, blights, sins, crimes, ineptitudes, pains, and problems, before my own. I fight your battles and trumpet your triumphs, as if they were my own. I prioritize your success, your fame, your family, your challenges, all before my own. Yes, i even play the fool, the donkey to bear the brunt of your hardship, some (most) time without your acknowledged gratitude. I'm the comforter you can lean on, who'd absorb your toxic drainage, the ugliness that you squeegee off of that facade, the sluice for which your sins and secrets are bathed away, pissed away, to be hidden from them who judge you…

My chagrin is masked by a veneer of upward-mobility and glass-half-full perspective, that, after 25 years, has worn thin, revealing in some places, a frail, timid, shivering man-child, hugging his ashen knees to his naked chest, dying

from a lack of truth, light, and Love...
Indeed, sitting here in this concrete and steel tomb, unnaturally cold, perpetually empty, i came to embody my habitat, disgusted by the reflection in the mirror. I found myself becoming more and more distant, loathing even my own company, taunted by an immoral inner voice...is this why the caged bird sings?
So i'm giving up, giving in. i'm screaming uncle!
I don't like it here.
I want to go...away.
I'm collecting my refund, my once indigent investment, and i'm expecting a return reflective of my penchant for surviving the odds. I was twelve for cryin' out loud! I could barely decide whether to shower every day, let alone what i'd expected to do with the rest of my life...the future is not something you can decide with a whiff of the armpits... I'm going to a life of bright multi-colors, liquid yellows, floral greens...where each day brings with it its own soundtrack...
where love is one God, one woman, one life...
I'm going to find forever.
There was a time when I had thought that I had believed that i didn't care if i lived or died. I even entertained a notion that as long as i was notorious for being evil, well then at least i'm relevant. I mean, you can't spell "infamous" without 'famous'. Right?
"I'd rather rule in hell, than serve in heaven", quoted from Paradise Lost, once was my motto, my mantra...
now, as i sit here at this indescribably cold desk, staring out of the frost-painted slit of a window, anticipating the next flow of syntax, now, i realize the absurdity of such a maxim. With no one to turn to, no one to cry to, this is hell.

In my pseudo-genetic make-up of gangsta-warrior-gladiator,
i've forgotten **how** to cry.
THIS is my hell...
I'm soon going to slough and scrape and shed this contemptible layer, this repulsive coating of grime from myself and leave it in the gutter...
...and i'm not looking back...
...it's over...i'm over...
For-ever free...i'm going home.

"Label me a success, I made the switch,
Retired from a life that never gave me sh-t..."
—Tupac

Circa 2012

Writer's Insight

My suicide note. Me vs Me. Creator against creature.

As I drew nearer to my realization that I couldn't be successful in life by holding close my previously learned negative core values, it also became painfully obvious that I had to essentially kill my former self and reclaim the identity that I was birthed to be. I designed and manifested the monster that I wanted the world to fear, without the forethought that a day would come when I would desire to be loved.

Freedom without fear is the essence of love...

If It Wasn't For Prison...

I'd be a lost soul, consoled by hate, cold and irate, stumblin'
thru a garden of stone;
Alone, reminiscin', sheddin' tears for the stolen years, the peers;
ignorant to death, yet aware that I'm near;
Blessin' my beer, sweatin', recitin' the Lord's prayer;
I know that God never gives a man more than he can bear…

> But If It Wasn't For Prison…

I wouldn't be a man, not just in the definite sense, but the man
that I am;
Standin' alone on my own two, mature to capacity;
Responsible, no longer naive to he who mastered me;
I fight back pensively, not passively, or dastardly;
Blastin' he who led me disastrously, and actually…

> If It Wasn't For Prison…

I'd be a statistic of anotha kind;
not in a mortal malaise, cauz the bullet left me paralyzed;
Blind and catatonic, non-responsive and shocked;
Who'da thought there'd be a downside to survivin' a gunshot…?
"Mind over matter", "Time heals all wounds";
Benevolent cliches fall short when you cain't move…

> Cauz, If It Wasn't For Prison…

Who knows where I'd be? Maybe President of the Free, or Chief Resident M.D.;
It's pleasant to think about - heaven and paradise;
But we fail to realize - to gain we must sacrifice,
"Ask and ye shall receive", i sought and he deceived,
Purged into an abyss of liars, sinners, and thieves...

(2002)

> ### Writer's Insight
>
> In 2002, I had been inside just about 11 years. I was in High Desert State Prison in Susanville, California. By far, one of the worst prisons in the Golden State. I was really honing my skills as a rapper and poet, taking on a variety of styles and subjects, trying to discover my own voice. I don't have very many of my pieces from back then, but the ones that remain, I cherish dearly.

Am I Invisible?

AM I INVISIBLE? OR IS EVERYBODY BLIND?
Am I just a body-less voice emanating from ethereal nothingness? Does my heart not break for Boston? For Aurora? Do the shattered shards of my heart not gleam beneath the radiance of Newtown's essence?

AM I INVISIBLE? OR IS EVERYBODY BLIND?
Can you not see me?! Not the tattoos and battle scars. Not the deformed, disfigured, and distorted image that you caught a glimpse of in passing, thru your averted glances, staring thru me, as if you don't acknowledge me, I won't exist…LOOK AT ME!! Please?
Pleas ignored…Denied…Unheard?

AM I INVISIBLE? OR IS EVERYBODY BLIND?
Would you…just notice me? I'm no ghost or phantom, I'm real. Please don't be afraid.
Can't you…feel me?
I"M RIGHT HERE!!!

AM I INVISIBLE? ARE YOU BLIND?
I'm as real as my mother's youngest son, my son's only father, as real as my grandbabies' Pop'Pop!

AM I INVISIBLE?
When I smile at you, I get blank stares in answer.
ARE YOU BLIND?
Is it fear? Am I the spook you see in your darkest dreams?
And if so, is that my fault?
I CHANGED MY WALK.
I CHANGED MY DEMEANOR.
AM I STILL THE MONSTER THAT YOU FEAR MOST?!
nah, 'cause that'd mean that you could see me…
Look, well, listen…I've been a gangster, a killer, a drug dealer, a crook…

A rebel, a fool, a savage, a beast…

A racist, a kidnapper, a murderer…
I've been brainwashed and programmed to hate and abhor the Who's What's & Where's. Not so much the Why, but definitely, yes, DEFINITELY, the How!
I HATED my enemies! I hated Each, Any, and Every-Thing that kept me from moving forward, upward, and onward. Everything that kept me stagnant…from growing…from progressing.

From loving, learning, living…enjoying.

I hated with a passion that which kept me from knowing happyness…And kept me angry and miserable and furious. I took a vow to destroy my enemies, the object of my utmost hate…

And I almost did it. I would've done it!

But I realized, sadly, that I was everything that I hated.
I was my own worst enemy. I was him who was in my own way.

The Beast.

The Monster.

The Fool.
But I did it. I scraped up the courage from the dregs of my conscience, and I killed him.
Well, the him who was me when I didn't know the me that I am now.
Standing here.
Begging to be seen, to be felt, to...Be.
Acknowledge me!!

ARE YOU ALL BLIND? OR AM I INVISIBLE?
I stand before you, more than mere words, as some**BODY** who feels the unforgiving burden of being unforgiven…
Stumbling beneath the weight of guilt, for the atrocities I've birthed with ignorant intentions, with the sinfully sinister bliss of a monster begging for redemption..
I'm not *INVISIBLE*.
SEE me…
HEAR me…
FEEL me…
Please…
…or are you BLIND?

Written in 2013

Writer's Insight

I still remember how hideous I felt when for the first time that I had begun to see real transformation in my personal life, I was faced with the reality that internal change isn't externally acknowledged…

I had enrolled in college, I had separated myself from my former criminal coterie; I was speaking differently, thinking differently, performing differently.

Yet, the treatment as an indentured servant was all the same.

I was still, in the eyes of the blind, the beast, the monster, the wretched of the earth.

And if I wasn't, then I was invisible - my efforts to be better, to be a success story, to be one less body to be counted…none of it registered.

I might as well have been invisible.

A View Outside The Window

I see the sunshine shining, breaking thru the grayest clouds
Peep how - the blue skies rejoice - the satin breeze seems proud
No Autumn rainfall or amber sunshowers
Just the mesmerizing rhythm of the swaying sunflowers
Close your eyes - envision the postcard picturesque scene, so serene
It's like, the essence of every hue magnifies the unseen
How every fallen leaf settles into a quilted mosaic
A blanket of daffodils covers up half a hill, displayin'
The capacity of nature's tenacity
This has to be a preview of better days - a glimpse of Heaven's tapestry
Morning dew glistens, making a spider's web a dreamcatcher
My mind becomes a whirlwind thinking of themes to name this scene after
Red Robins parlay - Hey! While Blue Jays get their songs right
Butterflies flutter by - anxious for nothing - life's a long flight…

September 2007

Writer's Insight

Tehachapi. California Correctional Institution. 2007.

I had been to this prison 2 times prior to this stint. Each time that I was there, I found myself in the hole (Ad-Seg) for either something I had done, was about to do, or had nothing whatsoever to do with.

This time particularly was the latter.

I was brought to the hole under an investigation that required a sweep of alleged gang leaders.

Once more, I found myself in an empty cell, living conditions at the barest minimum. My thoughts and ideas were my only tried and true confidants.

Outside of the back window was a hill - wilderness - survival at its most minute measure.

And yet…

…there was so much more to behold.

The Diamond

The diamond is one of the most coveted gems in all the world. Yet, as we behold the diamond in all its splendor and beauty, how would the diamond, if it could, see herself? Would the diamond see her own magnificent qualities, as the world does…? Or would she see herself, still, as a maleficent lump of carbon?

When (Colored) Boys Become Men
<the prelude>

When "colored" boys become men, childish appetites will no longer drive their desires. Schoolyard promises will diminish upon graduation, upon maturity, upon manhood mannerisms. The oaths that we took way back then will evaporate along with the very breath that those words clung to.

Just vapor in the wind…

How does one nurture a culture of ***physical*** men who have the psychological development of ***pre-teens*** and ***pre-pubescent*** adolescents?

The blatant response is: **YOU DON'T !!**

Yet, we do.

Not only do we nurture a culture of grown men with boyish behaviors, we allow other cultures to nurture, encourage, and exploit our arrested cultural development! This will **STOP** when our boys become men.

"When I was a child I spoke as a child, I understood as a child, I thought as a child, but, when I became a man, I put away childish things…" 1 Corinthians 13:11

When Boys Become Men

When Boys become Men…
…They will no longer be influenced by destructive poeticisms, malignant images of murder and mysogyny; manipulated by mismotivations of blood money "by any means". They will no longer forfeit their precious breath for the artificial oxygen of materialism and blacktop bravado…

When Boys become Men…
…Their women will be regarded as royal; their daughters will be doted upon, refined as the rarest of jewels, cultivated and cultured as pearls, which came as dirt and dust, sand and sediment, manifesting into the magnificence to be cherished as the matriarchs of our tomorrows…

When Boys become Men…
…They will love one another as they love themselves, having first learned to appreciate their uniqueness, to accept their imperfections, to acknowledge and account their flaws, because THEM Men are HUE-Men, abstract and valuable. And when they see that in themselves, they will see themselves in each other. 'Cauz L-O-V-E is Life's Only Valid Enjoyment…

…When Boys become Men…
…They will no longer see each other as paper targets to be punched and perforated, pierced

and punctured; they will no longer role play as predator and prey, a blackened silhouette peered at thru the cross hairs of self-hate, self-destruction, and self-degeneration…

…When Boys become Men…
…They will rightfully reclaim their roles in society as the "Misters", and not the mis's. And, I DO NOT mean to be understood as referring to the female pronoun. NO! The mis's I'm referring to are: MISanthropists, MISogynists, MISologists, and MISoneists! Cauz, see - misanthropism is the HATRED or MISTRUST of humankind…misogynism is the HATRED of women…misologism is the HATRED of Reason, Argument, and Enlightenment…and, misoneism is the HATRED or FEAR of change or innovation. When our Boys become Men, they will no longer be MIStrusted, MISTAKEN, MISeducated, MISGUIDED, or MISTREATED. No longer will our Men be MIScreant or MISfits. They will be the MISTERS - the Men - that they are supposed to be…

…When Boys become Men…

…They will no longer merchandise their morality to the highest bidder; pawn off their principles as if unnecessary, herald our juvenile delinquency as though it were honorable…! When Men put away their childish things they will no longer subscribe to the vows they took as PRE-PUBESCENT pawns, played as expendable, portrayed as items to be exchanged for someone else's gain…

…When Boys become Men…
…They will recognize their authenticity, they will BELIEVE that they are not a Hollywood caricature of SUB-urban conditions. No!! When Boys become Men, then Men will become Leaders and Teachers and Chairmen… They will become Prophets and Poets and Griots… They will become Kings…and, Obama's and Chavez's…and Men of Valor…

…When Boys become Men..
…They will stand up!! Claim the

AUDACITY to be AUTHENTIC!
Don't be the Blah-Blah replica of yesterday's festering regrets!!
Stand Up and Be Men!
Don't ACT Like Men, BE Men!

Writer's Insight

I was in Vacaville, California Medical Facility, when I wrote this. After spending the first 26 years on maximum security battlefields across the state, I had been conditioned to perceive things a certain way. I could see or hear or feel an authentic person's presence just by the way that they conducted themselves, by the way that they walked or by who they associated with. As well, I could spot the artificial ones just as easily using the same measure. Even after I had long since retired my membership to that subculture, I still breathed in undertones of the lifestyle. It's probably why I was able to reach some of the youth that I had become a mentor to. The unreachable and unteachable, as they had been deemed by others, would come to me for guidance, to vent and be heard, to listen and be taught. I could only offer the advice that my peers and I had wished that we had been given back then. Child soldiers are only as valuable as their ignorance allows. When I was taught to think for myself and became aware of my own self-worth, I taught my equals and multiplied my value.

A lot of our misdirected youth only need someone to give them the distraction they need to focus.

Ironic.

Confession of a Compassionate Felon #2

"He was only six years old when he experienced injustice for the first time. Not only was it a social and moral injustice, but a horrible personal atrocity. He was attacked and assaulted by a boy seven years his superior, in a room full of their peers, each who, for one excuse or another did absolutely nothing to prevent the affront on his precious childhood. To add humiliation to hurt, his parents and siblings reacted with apathy and indifference, leaving his six-year-old's calculations to render himself to blame for what had happened to him.

The years that succeeded him weren't any less brutal. He bounced from home to home to apartment to relative's couch-bed. He left one school for another, staying long enough to learn new acquaintance's surnames before traversing along to the next vacancy. His parents divorced, his home was broken like his little boy heart, and the only family that he'd never felt membership with was soon split into mathematical figures.

He felt lost. He felt irrelevant..unnecessary..unacceptable.

Soon he sought the embrace of the fellow-forsaken, welcomed into a fraternity of surrogate siblings who'd all felt, in some way, destiny-deprived, yet, driven to overcome by every necessary means…"

His abrupt pause left the scholastic audience clutching barely the unexpressed thought. His narration teased the tickled ears, enticing his peers' famished imaginations, only to leave an ellipsis as the breadcrumbs for which to follow.

Even his teacher was over-the-top impressed with his style

of storytelling. His vocabulary far-surpassed that of the other juveniles in his age group, far out measuring most of the adults in his under-served community. Yet, his confident eloquence captivated her to the core of her inner bookworm.

Yet, Jester felt as inadequate, as out of place as he'd always felt when asked to share his written sentiments. Whether his stories were autobiographical or fiction, his listeners never could tell. Nor would he.

"Jester, uh, that was…I mean, the way that you speak, it's…" Ms. Markle was tactless hardly never, yet, she could barely match the proper predicate with its subject. "Um, would you like to finish? I-I mean, is there *more*?"

Jester scanned the faces of his classmates, searching for justification for his punctuated halt to storytime, finding instead eager expressions, each anticipating a satisfying conclusion for the beleaguered protagonist.

The truth was, Jester, at thirteen years old, was a storyteller beyond his years in wisdom. He possessed the spirit of a village griot, one, who, not merely *told* stories, but, *wove* fascination with knowledge, *married* rhythm with imagery, and breathed new life into parable-telling of old.

"There's more…just, not ready yet."

He sat down in his seat, cracked his knuckles as if an exclamation, then folded his single page of prose into his faded red folder of unshared treasures.

It wasn't as if his story wasn't ready to be told, or even that it was still unfinished. Jester knew that such a jewel cast before an unappreciative audience would be trampled underfoot. It was *they* who were the not ready.

Outside of the classroom, the afternoon sun weighed warmth atop Jester's head and neck. It was early June, his third favorite month, and his second spent inside of the isolated chaos that was Ostenwald Juvenile Facility. He hated being locked up. He hated that incarceration was a viable remedy for crime deterrence, much like a frontal lobotomy was the preferred remedy for a sinus headache. He hated that there was a need for such places as Ostenwald, that there existed in 21st century America, a machine that churns the morally poor and emotionally impoverished out in historic figures, creating disenfranchised dregs and delinquents, deplorables and degenerates, dogs that eat other dogs over crumbs that are brushed from the mouths of the master-minded.

Above all, Jester *hated* that after everything that history has exposed; the abhorrent atrocities, the current catastrophes over class and race, the stratagems being employed to ensure future mass disasters, in which the earth-toned majority would suffer terribly, when it was all done and said, the fittest dog would still be shot down before the fall of the final crumb.

But, as Jester also acknowledged, it wasn't as if the juveniles that he was chained up with were all innocent as bliss. Some, if not, most, have committed some atrocious crimes. Exploits that far surpass the adult criminal-minded. Whether willing participants - crime scene instigators - with a fervor for the fatal and ferocious; or, the rat pack, kill or be killed, "I won't take it anymore", rebels without a cause, every minor within these lead paint-covered, cinder block walls was a danger to themselves and to their respective communities.

Jester was definitely a threat to all things breathing and being. At eleven years old, when most boys were obsessing over puberty and times tables, he was strategizing about a move that would facilitate a significant alteration in the lives of those who deserved it most…

My Light

I was adrift in the nothingness of darkness
Cloaked by the fuzzy warmth of emptiness
No light No sound No anything
I couldn't tell if i was laying down or standing up
Suspended ascension…or, descent
Virtual purgatory
The torture of absolute silence would bore thru me
Far beyond the mere sense of sound
I felt it
But, its all that i felt
In this utter abyss of eternal midnite, i felt nothing
I wasn't numb…
…i'd pray for numbness…
…the glorious sting from every stab of the jagged shards of broken glass and rusted thumbtacks and crusted barbs of fish hooks tearing at my forsaken flesh…
…i'd pray for it
To feel alive again
One more chance
Just one more
And i did…at least I think I did…I think I think I did
I screamed and I whispered
To Him…or Her or, Them way way up above
Please please please please please please, et cetera
Let me feel again
Let me see hear taste touch smell again

And then it came
The light appeared unexpectedly
I felt it more than I saw it…
…Its warmth Its vibrancy Its brilliancy Its love
Then, it touched me It pulled at me It wanted me to come and I wanted to go…
…so It pulled and I pushed and I pushed and I…held back

Fear

What if i pushed too hard in my urgency to be free of this living death
And I pushed her away…
Yes, it was a her
She
My Light
I smelled her - a melange of myrrh and sunflower and…happyness
Certain i'm not how I knew what it was at first but love (and joy and ecstasy) is the explanation I received in the comprehensive part of my brain…
…or soul…
…or spirit…
My light
I love her
And she pulled at me as i pushed away from the NothingEmptyness that had enveloped my life…
…or existence…
…or whatever it was that i wasn't when I was not feeling
She rescued me
My light
I love her

30 May 2012

Writer's Insight

I was in Corcoran State Prison when I wrote this. Level 4, still swimming against the current of change. I was 37 years old, 21 years in, and still trying to figure myself out.

It would be a few months later that I made my announcement to the populace that I was officially retiring from all association with criminality, all affiliation with urban militarism, and embracing my once forfeited position as a civilian.

And I did.

"My Light" is a description of what & who I clutched closely while I was struggling to remain intact inside emotionally and mentally. My closest connection then was a beautiful human being from Torino; someone who arrived unexpectedly, enhanced and broadened my perspective of self and the world that revolved around me, then eventually evaporated into the ether...

A Fotograf 1980

Two little boys - spittin' images of innocence
Faces fat with happy smiles of bygone birthday wishes
Curly-haired heads smellin' like playground sand and Coast soap
Twin cowboys - chaps over Tuff Skins, vests atop superhero t-shirts
Five candles aflame, waiting 'til the merry-go-round has lost its appeal, to be blown out
Two little boys, pistols drawn, faces frowned, laughter abandoned
Sing happy birthday

Written:
19 November '19

I Was Raised By…

I was raised by my mother with the highest regard
Taught me love in the home, kept me solid on the boulevard
French Toast from scratch, grilled cheese after skool
Despised the notion that her youngest was a fool
"Baby, don't be a mark, hit first & hit HARD.."
28 years since I left her, yet memories don't scar…

I was raised by my father, convinced myself that he didn't bother
Not to see me or hear me, not to teach me, not to reach out…
Yeah, he showed me how to ignore, how to abhor what I didn't understand
How to punch what wouldn't listen, but, ironically, i miss him…

I was raised by rhythm & lyrics, by break-beats & loops
From Run-DMC 2 Whodini, Ice-T had me at "6 In The Mornin'" ironing my jeans before school
I was the boy wonder of breakdancin', studying *Beat Street* techniques
Then the west coast brought Ozone & Turbo, *Breakin'* at Venice Beach
'87 I started bangin', "Gangsta, Gangsta" was my soundtrack
Couldn't imagine what this life would be like if I'd never found rap…

December 2019

Writer's Insight

This poem was birthed from a challenge made in a creative writing group in California Medical Facility, Vacaville. The facilitator was an established author, a poet, photographer, and novelist. He wanted to see where everyone was artistically, so he wrote a sentence on the white board, a single simple line:
"Who Raised You?"

Thoughts Off The Top Of My Head

Accentuate my raps wit' finga snaps and handclaps
Deodorant caps an' toothbrush taps, my flows neva lapse
Encode raps wit messages, hieroglyphic in essence,
Its pyrotechnics, my methods light up the club…
Poetically deadly, lyrics ignite, im spittin' flammable fluid
Line up a crew of rhyme shootaz, i go Lion like Lucious…
Homie, they foolish, they think blind people stupid,
Dey' insecure in their hearts, so I shoot thru 'em like cupid…
Lyrical pugilist I punch lines,
Bonecrusher, go manic on mics, it's in my bloodline…
My heart is..desperately wicked, its deceptive and toxic,
I paid my **LIFE** for my crimes, and now my change is the profit…
Peep the prose of the prophet painted precise as Picasso,
Walk by faith, but these premonitions keep makin' me hostile,
On the verge of impossible, drama thickens the plot,
Odds against me or not, I'ma give it my shot,
For Biggie, Nipsey, and 'Pac..if Black lives are precious
Then **STOP** killin' each other, the world jus' don't respect us..
(And) That's a rational nexus, but my perspective perplexes,
I'm tryna turn this MESS into a MESSage….
But, when it's all done and said,

These jus' the thoughts off the top of my head…
I see danger and i chuckle, my knees never buckle,
I walk thru the Valley of Death crackin' my knuckles,
I'm a conqueror, but so much more,
Blood-stained banner, Aunt Jemima style, knees on the floor;
Help me Father see the signs, i'm third-eye blind,
I cain't lie, doubt can be a wicked bully sometimes,
I got the faith of a chronic seed, sub-atomically,
I manifest into a man that's blessed, true anomaly…
Although, ironically, i used to think that God was a myth,
I thought the devil rocked a Prada skirt, and death was a gift…
I was a gangland phenomenon, hidin' behind a mask like it was Comic-Con,
Had the masses all breakin' fast, like it was the last night of Ramadan..!!
But now a righteous path is all i'm on….
No more Joker Face, the Lok'est Souljah is in a sober place,
Searchin' for amor, found **AGAPE** spread all over space…
Scribbled lines from my PaperMate, concentrates,
Criminal contemplates, into critical conversations…WAIT!!

STIGMA

Stigma - a mark or token of infamy, disgrace, or reproach; ARCHAIC: a mark burned into the skin of a criminal or slave; a brand tattoo indicating slave or criminal status

When a slave is given Freedom, who is it that declares him free?
Is it society? Or himself?
Is bondage (slavery) more mental than physical? More emotional than rational?
Who decides?
If a slave declares him/herself a free **Human Being**, yet, society, as a mass, still sees him/her as anything but **Free, Human, & Being**...who's view really matters?

The Other Side of Life

What makes a lion, a lion?
Is it the roar of a thousand thunders? The measure of his pride?
His majestic characteristics?
Is it his fangs, his claws, his mane?
On the contrary, is a lion without fangs and claws still the King of the Jungle?
What then is it that makes a lion, a lion?

There once was a young lion, a juvenile, the prince of his pride, who, in his zeal for kingdom relevancy, killed a young, innocent doe - not for food, nor for sport, but simply because he could. His reckless disregard for all things living was often applauded and acclaimed amongst his peers. However, the chauvinism displayed by his abhorrent act caught the attention of an authority that he disdained with utter contempt.

One day, a day that he somehow felt was looming, inevitable, fateful, the young lion suddenly found himself surrounded by the alien authority, separated from his clan, and taken away. He believed, somewhere deep in the beat of his breast, that he would someday be called to account for his un-natural slaughter of the precious doe.

An eye for an eye, a tooth for a tooth, and a pound of flesh was the required price for a soul according to the laws of the wildlife. The sentence that he received, however, much to his surprise, was an existence - a living, breathing hell - far worse than death.

Having now been captured and indicted, he was imprisoned, tried, and ultimately condemned to a period of re-conditioning. Despite his feral refusal to be emotionally remolded and intrinsically transformed, the young lion's anarchism faded, his rage and resistance reluctantly waned. In the clarifying moments of despair, he realized that his desire to be reunited with his family had far superseded his ambition to be re-established with his pride.

After a span of time that had brought the lion much closer to his end than to his beginning, he had been deemed suitable for emancipation and allowed release back into the wild; the immoral wasteland that he had not only forgotten, but essentially had forgotten him. He had been de-fanged and de-clawed. His once terra-trembling rebel's roar had been reduced to a hoarse, hollow, humbled bellow.

"How will I survive?", he pensively pondered.

His entire incarcerated existence had been catered: his every meal had been provided and served; his every duty and responsibility pacified.

Though he once fought fiercely for valor, oftentimes, for vanity, he now found himself in the kill or be killed wilderness - unarmed and unimposing - no longer brash and brawny, instead, bowed and benign, as he feared, to be vanquished by the other side of life.

Writer's Insight

I wrote this after I had been found suitable for parole. I was awaiting release back into society after nearly three decades behind ashen gray walls and iron-enforced enclosures. In just a countdown of a few weeks I would be walking out reformed and restructured.

I was apprehensive, to put it mildly, didn't really know what to expect. I convinced myself that I was prepared for whatever, but the truth was, I didn't have a clue as to what to anticipate. I tried to remind myself that it was just like going to a new prison, a different yard, same rules…

But it wasn't like that at all. Prison has structure, foundation, unyielding policies. Society is…free and foreign and forlorn. Kinda like I would be…

AN UNNECESSARY LIFE

Tell me that you love me…Please?
Somebody? Anybody? Please?
Why won't you look at me?
Is it my smile? The way I dress?
Am I too dark? My skin? My humor? My soul?
Am I too white? White is blank is passionless is…without life.
Would I be better off if…?
Would you even miss me?
I want to be loved. Don't I deserve it?
Can I be relevant to someone?
Extraordinary, even tho' sometimes I feel extra-ordinary?
Am I mistaken? Was / the mistake?
Tell me I'm wanted, needed, desired,
PLEEEAAASSSEE, tell me that I matter.
Anyone?
Does nothing matter at all?
Or, am I unnecessary…?

The padded silence of Rian's tap-tap-tapping on her touchscreen tablet, paused pregnantly, leaving her somber prose unfinished. She'd never fancied herself a poet, but her mood, the relentless downpour of melancholy, prompted her to emote her deepest, diary-like sentiments.

However, this less-than-casual catharsis was more than just a random tweet, more profound than some multi-text sent out into the ether. Its intimacy revealed something much more abysmal.

Rian felt alone.

In a world of six billion, she was the alien among the populace. Anonymous and lonely, foreign and forlorn. Rian felt that she was unnecessary. At fourteen years old, with much uncharted
adventure before her, Rian had spent the last five thousand-plus days, seeking, searching for her connection to life, and the living, and... to love.

Her mother, Jade, was the essence of effervescence and beauty on the outside. Men fell before her feet, volunteering their very being as a traverse over mud puddles; their souls, they would gladly exchange for a parcel of her forbidden paradise. Rian's mom was the Cleopatra of their synthetic suburban community.

But for all the honey and skim-milk-skinniness that Jade proffered to the Viagra-vikings and Low-T Cro-Magnons, Rian knew that inside, her mom was despicably rotten, and irredeemably rancid. Jade was a toxic mish-mash of misery, who took her anger and disappointment and frustration and painful reluctance to accept the inevitability of natural progress of life, out on her kids.

Rian has a little sister also. The spry and spunky, seven year old, princess-in-the-works, the reality-t.v.-starling-waiting-to-be-discovered, Giovana. When she's not singing horrendously off-key, or dancing rhythm-lessly in front of Rian's full-length, closet-door mirror, she's somewhere being ignored and loathed, by the figure she calls "Mommy". That same "Mommy" who loathed and ignored and despised a then seven year old, Rian... And detested, denied, and devalued the ten year old Rian, when Jade's heart had been pummeled by a fugitive fling who'd promised her the world.

For her eleventh birthday, Rian didn't have a party. Instead, Jade gave Rian a piece of "candy" that she promised would make Rian feel happy and fuzzy and light, like a "catty-pillar". She then told Rian to go out and play. on the freeway overpass.

"You'll be able to fly and flutter like a butterfly, sweetie!", Jade had told Rian, reminiscent of the Evil Witch offering Snow White the poisoned apple.

Fortunately, Rian never made it beyond the back porch. She vomited violently, and then, blacked-out, sleeping unnoticed and neglected, until the next morning.

Once, Rian asked her mom why she didn't love her. Jade, ever the emblem of motherhood, answered Rian's query without a hint of saccharine. "Love you? Why, sweetheart, I don't even *like* you." That was yesterday.

This morning, when she arose from a sleepless night of wheezing sobs, and dry, tearless crying, and the deafening click-clack-clang of the jagged shard that rattled around inside of her shattered heart, Rian felt compelled to write a verse, a requiem, for her emotional malaise. She was giving in already to give up, convinced that she wasn't capable - or worthy - of being loved. *Unnecessary.* And now, as she sat lotus pose-like on her bedroom floor, the itchy, scratchy, tobacco-spit-brown shag carpet, brushing against her bare legs, Rian contemplated how it would end-

KNOCK-KNOCK-KNOCK

"Go away!" Rïan ordered angrily, her flow of dismal contemplation interrupted.

KNOCK-KNOCK-KNOCK

"GO away! Leave me ALONE!"

"But, Rian, I need you to help me with my fairy wings!" Giovana protested.
"PLEEEAAASSSEE?"

Rian reluctantly padded to the door and nearly snatched it off its hinges. She looked down into the almond-shaped, aquamarine eyes that stared back up at her, instantly disarming her fury, defusing her self-destruct mechanism.

Although she had only been contemplating how to end her poem, the unexpected distraction from Giovana gave her the remedy she'd needed. Looking down at her little sister, the pitiable, misassembled fairy's wings held in her tiny clutch, provided Rian the answers she'd sought.

Her life *was* very necessary.

Giovana's suffocating, supergirl-hug, and wide, toothy smile, was all the affirmation she needed.
"As a reward for helping a fairy, you get one free miracle! Anything you want!", Giovana squealed with glee.

Rian smiled, wiping away an errant tear.

"I already got it, kiddo."

Writer's Insight

April 2, 2013, I wrote this as a challenge to myself. I wanted to see if I could write a story from the perspective of someone that I wasn't accustomed to, a life that I've never lived. I mean, I could've chosen to create a character like Atticus Finch or Mr. Roark Is that really a challenge though? A pre-teen girl-child - unloved, unappreciated, unnecessary…but perspective is everything.

I Don't Know, Jus' Thinkin'...

Remember when we were in our childhood, when, for the most part, everyone was pretty much equal? I mean, we was all poor, or we was all jus' gettin' by, but for what it was worth, we were equally innocent and yet still unblemished by life. There was always that one child that was beloved by all - by the kids and parents, by the teachers and elders, even the bullies went a little less hard on him or her. This child wasn't particularly special or unique, they were just the beloved of the bunch.

And, there was always some significant event that would occur, be it a holiday, a birthday, or just a freaky Friday, when this child would receive something precious, a gift or a token of some achievement, something that the rest of the neighborhood children rarely, if ever, would receive. But, in true fashion, this child would come outside with his or her gift, would proudly display it for all to see, yet would also humbly allow all to partake, to handle, to caress, to share.

Not for the sake of gloating or boasting did this child do this, but because, in some innocent way, he or she felt a sense of general guilt for the have-nots and have-less that he/she found himself/herself surrounded with. The cherished gift would be passed around, fondled by every kind of prod and poke, it would be examined, dissected, and discussed; tossed this way and that, borrowed, begged for, and bartered with.

Yet, as this once adored gift lay at the feet of the beloved child, tattered and torn in myriad fragments, an almost indiscernible frame of what it once was, the child would simply return to the very essence of who he or she had always been; the silent, brooding, constantly contemplating, tear-smeared face between the shadows of the have-nots and the have-less.

I am that child, my life is that gift, and I am between the shadows of emotion and apathy.

Fourteen months later…

11/30/21

Writer's Insight

I remember writing this piece. It began as an inexpressible feeling that I had. I was free after thirty years of captivity, I should've still been riding that high 14, 15…24 months later.

Instead, I felt an overwhelming sense of guilt.

There were just so many people that wanted my time, just a piece, if I were willing. There was much that I wanted to do. And… there were voices in the wind that made me think that if I wasn't more charitable with my time - with myself - then, I didn't deserve to be free.

I was even told that I owed a lot of myself to the people that stuck by me while I was away!

Wait, what?!

My mother is the ONLY person who did NOT disappear for months and years at a time!

ONLY…

It is still difficult for me to share myself with a lot of people and family

Eau de Skidrow

It's an amalgam of human urine and raw doggy doo, the aroma of despair, spritz'd and mist'd, traipsed thru by passer-by and staggerer alike....body odor and halitosis mingle and make love to conceive a funk so assaulting upon the olfactory sensors, that it becomes in essence, an all-out affront to the six senses, yes, even the (un)common one....the spectrum is exceeded when sight, sound, taste, smell, and touch are shocked and awed by an unforeseen attack, a visceral overload of foot fungus and crotch rot; weeks worth of unwashed boxer briefs and long-since commando'd dungarees, piss-stained, poop-smeared, and sludge-smudged...the end-of-summer heat wave just bakes and burnishes the macabre mash-up into a flagrant fragrance, an indescribable tastetouchsmellfeelheard gumbo of icky melancholy....
how thankful i am for soap and water

October 4, 2020

Writer's Insight

I was, again, only freed just a few weeks prior to writing this. 29+ calendars had been flipped through and discarded before I was finally liberated.

San Francisco's Tenderloin District is still a much greener pasture in comparison to the unquenchable thirst that is the soul-suppressing hellfire of bondage and confinement within California's prison industrial complex.

I don't miss it.

I won't ever return.

Not ever.

An Effort For Heaven

In one of the most remote spots in all the globe, located in the tropic tundra, where the Isle of Sumatra and the Yucatan Peninsula caress, just shy of the intimate intrusion of the Java Coastline, juts a mammoth proportion of stone, a jagged tooth of concentrated amazement, known to most as the Canopy of Grace. It is said that on the plateau of this impossible mountain rests the House of God, open and free to all who enter.

Ezell Fish, a 40-something, "carpe diem, conquer the world!" adventurist, has committed himself to the most arduous task: scaling the sheer, marble-slick face of the mountain, determined to prove himself worthy to enter God's rest, securing himself a place in heaven.

Ezell, who's self-confidence is astronomically immeasurable, rests on the undeniable fact that he has already humbled every massive height under the sun. From Kilimanjaro to the mythic Mount Olympus, Ezell holds every record, and every laurel, for his granite-grappling abilities. There isn't a ridge or range on any continent that he hasn't triumphed. His every boast is in himself, his work, and his autonomy. When it comes to vanquishing the vertex of life, Ezell Fish claims to be the elitist of the elite.

On the day of days that has chosen Ezell to scale God's foothold, after ceremoniously taping his fingers, chalking his hands, inspecting his harness and ropes for knits, knots, and notches, Ezell mutters a quick litany of praise and worship to his deity du jour, digs in, and begins his ascent.

Well into his climb, at an altitude where anything with featherless wings gets vertigo, the skirt of fog was unusually dense, as if the very clouds of the mid-morning sky had descended to cheer Ezell on. Between periodic breaks to quench his thirst, to replenish electrolytes, to give respite to his physical equipment, Ezell reminded himself that progress is a process. He must keep climbing.

Six days, seventeen hours, and nine minutes of toil and temptation to quit, a torn fingernail and calloused callouses, rendered Ezell's compensation in full. The glory of God's holy habitat was spectacular to behold. He could utter nothing coherent, or lucid, yet, his tears of joy and awe expressed sufficiently what adjectives wouldn't.

With temerity re-established, Ezell boldly approached the massive entranceway. A wondrous, winding path, paved with jewels and stones of unimaginable cut and clarity, colors of such vivid complexion that they were nearly hypnotic, beckoned Ezell forward. For as far as his eyesight could dare, Ezell saw grass, almost as liquid as it was lush; as green as pre-Adam Eden preserved.

On impulse, Ezell ran his battered hands through the majestic meadow, his palms resting atop each attentive shaft. Be it inspiration or invention, Ezell felt the amazing sensation of being spiritually embraced through his fingertips. The blades of grass ministered to his soul, witnessing to his every nerve-ending, a choir of supernatural savannah.

The sky, an astounding impression of blue, seemed - *felt* - closer, Ezell continued along, comfortably coerced by the perfect temperature, until he reached the colossal double-doors of God's tabernacle.

Ezell found it remarkable that the doors, though, monstrous in size, and, no doubt, in weight, were absolutely as unadorned, and, well, plain, as anything he'd find anywhere back home.

Still, he had his reward to claim.

Ezell rang the doorbell.

No churchy bells, as one would expect. Not even a Christmas carol-y jingle.

Just a simple ding-dong.

After a well-impatient thirty seconds, Ezell pressed the doorbell again.

Still, no response.

Ezell rings and rings with such succession that even after he'd stopped pushing the button, the ding-donging kept going until it caught up.

Embarrassed at his obvious display of impiety at the home of the Almighty, Ezell resigns to give up.

Then he remembers his folly. With a demure giggle at his expense, Ezell knocks on the door.

Without a squeak or squeal, the gargantuan doors swung open. The freshest, most pure air, breezed across his face as an absent-minded kiss.

A soft, nearly still voice spoke.

"***Who are you who dares to enter the Holy House of Jehovah?***"

Ezell was taken aback. He half-expected to be met with a thundering voice, Wizard of Oz-style.

"Uh, sir-, Father...uh, it's me, Ezell Fish. I climbed up the side of your mountain to enter into your place of rest. I did what nobody else could do. I did the work, *I* perfected the skills, and *I* successfully did the very best!"

Ezell soberly realized how emphatic he was in his self-aggrandizing.

"Uh, Father Lord God Jehovah, sir...I *earned* my place in your paradise. Pl-Please, let me in."

There was a momentary pause that seemed to span an infinity.

Ezell felt an icy trickle of perspiration meander down his back.

"***Ezell,***" the Ethereal Whisper began, "***indeed, you have worked, and you have toiled, you climbed the sheer, rocky cliffs of My holy mountain, all with the deepest desire to enter into paradise. In saying so, you are correct. But, look to your left, Ezell.***"

Ezell Fish averted his gaze to peer over his left shoulder. It took his body two seconds to catch up with his visual shift, but in half the time, the consummation of belief and reality birthed understanding.

There, to Ezell's amazement, and horror, stood a multitude of people, thousands upon thousands! There were men and women; young, old, and middle-wise, of every orientation, ideology, and conviction. Some rested on the grassy plateau, spent from their taxing ascent. Others, ever the servants of dead works, were assisting those who were just reaching the top.

Ezell was devastated. He couldn't wrap his mind around what was so patently obvious.

Turning again to the Omniscient voice, Ezell sought clarity. How had he not seen all of these people before? How did he miss what had clearly been right before his eyes the whole time? How could he not-

"***Ezell,***" the Voice interrupted, "***now look to your right.***"

With unpleasant reluctance, Ezell turned. His eyes could hardly accept the brilliance of power and light, the undeniable solicitation of love being emitted preternaturally. What he witnessed took his breath away and brought him to body-wracking sobs.

What Ezell saw, off in the distance, stood a straight, narrow, but obviously sturdy bridge. Hundreds of thousands of people traversed this overpass effortlessly, jubilant in the gracious accommodation made on their behalf, to enter into heaven. Every person on earth was represented, each gender, and every nationality, except, there was no designation of color, no preference of appearance. Everybody was equally acceptable.

"But, I don't understand, God. What have I missed?" The tears made gray streaks through his dust-caked face.

The Voice, as patient, and, as peaceful, as any could expect, spoke to Ezell.

"My Son paid a tremendous price to build a bridge that would lead all who trust, through faith in Him, directly to paradise. You, like the majority of the world, have chosen to try to earn your wages through toil and labor. You were obviously blinded by your own concepts of heaven and how to enter, instead of listening to My Son, Who has said, 'I am the Way, the Truth, and the Life...'

"The bridge was built so that you wouldn't have to break your back trying to do the impossible - work your way into heaven."

Ezell wept inconsolably

"So, what now, Lord? For all of us who have arrived the hard way, can we stay in heaven?"

"This is not heaven, Ezell. You see," the Voice explained, *"there are many ways to God, but there is only One Way that leads to Heaven."*

The End.

Writer's Insight

In 2012 I surrendered my membership to the anti-lifestyle of gang activity and the all-encompassing foolishness that it drags with it. In 2013, I began attending church. Immediately, I felt as if I had discovered what had been missing from my existence, that very element that I had been chasing after forever.

As I grew stronger in my walk with my Lord and Savior, and as my understanding and enlightenment expanded, I realized that I had been given the irrevocable gifts of preaching and teaching, of helping and administration, and that my abilities and talents had been enhanced to better serve the spreading of the gospel.

"An Effort For Heaven" came about as I had been explaining to a crowd of skeptics that entrance into paradise can't be earned on merit or earthly effort…it isn't earned at all.

Justa Letchu Know

For every one rotten bitch, there's two good women.
I recognize, tho', i'll admit, there's hard times given,
Livin' thru agony, misery, neglect, and double-standards,
Respect to all my solid sistas, strivin' for answers..
Seekin' remedies...it's in your Khemistry to organize, you want solutions,
To fix our fragile nation in the depths of this confusion…
I swear to Life, your strength is amazin'(!)
Breathin' life into my dreams, when all i feel is frustration;
Tell me, sista, what is your motivation…? Inspire me…
In spite of all the stuff we put you thru you still support your man, entirely,
Givin' your hearts entirety…and still find time
To be a dime, Girl, your shine's unreal..!!
That natural glow compliments your appeal, no need to be,
Artificial wit' me, cauz, you' for us, I am We…!
It's Interdependency, my innermost tendency,
Is to give her the keys to Heaven, delivered on a bended knee…
But, this precious soliloquy is a whisper beneath the raucous
If the man I am won't **STAND UP***, and breathe for our daughters*
I just had ta letcha know, Sis, for all that you do,
No-Thing compares to you….

Writer's Insight

I was in Tehachapi State Prison, 2008…I was listening to Michelle Obama talk about her support of her husband, Barack Obama's desire to run for the Presidency.

In spite of whatever they had been going through personally, she set it all aside to support his otherwise impossible quest to be the first Black president of the United States.

I was in awe of her beauty, her intelligence, of her POWER…I was inspired! JUSTA LETCHU KNOW was written as an homage to the UnCommon Queens that my chauvinism and misogynistic conditioning had previously blinded me to.

Postmark From Paris

Dear Friend,

Hey stranger, what's good? I know it's been a while since I last wrote, but I hope this letter finds you in the best of health and staying positive, despite the circumstances. Believe me, homeboy, it gets better.

I know it tripped you out to see a postmark from Paris, huh? Yeah, I've been living here for about a year now. The journey that it took to get here was nothing short of miraculous, but it's waking up each day in the embrace of peace and unrestrained happiness that is truly the reward. I'm sure that sounds a bit trite, especially coming from me, but it's the truth, homeboy. There really is light at the end of the tunnel. You just have to keep marching forward. "Can't Stop! Won't Stop!"

Remember that?

So, what's new with you? How've you been treatin' life? How's the family? A few days before hopped on the plane to come here, I stopped by your mother's house to check on her, to see if she needed anything. You know moms! She had me cuttin' grass, pullin' weeds, and washin' windows! HAHAHA! I thought she might've needed some groceries or needed me to run an errand, and I ended up exhausted!

HAHAHA!

But I was happy to do it. It reminded me of the

time when we were thirteen and you had threatened to run away from home rather than spend your summer weekend doing chores. Moms said, "Go on and run away! It's just more work for him!"

I love you homeboy, but I was not about to do your chores!

HAHAHA!

Yeah, seriously though, I think about our childhood a lot. Well, I guess "childhood" would be the wrong word. Our adolescence went from pre-teens straight to pre-trial! Transferring from one lock-down facility to another, all the way into adulthood. And the crazy part of it all is that we wore it like a badge of honor! When we were fourteen and fifteen, we looked forward to going to juvenile hall! Then, if we graduated to camp and the youth authority, it was just more kudos! How ridiculous is that? We actually aspired to be the worst that we can be, to be notorious... and for what? Whose purpose do we serve by being locked up? Not our families. Definitely, not our families!

And if it's somehow in the best interest of the gang, or the "cause", or the movement, for us to be isolated and held captive, how come we aren't better off in the end? We make these on-the-spot, life-ruining decisions, or, at times have them made for us, mostly, I suppose, 'cause we never anticipated anything being long-term. Not even our own lives!

Hey, remember when my moms asked us what we wanted to be when we got older? I was stuck, staring down at the ground like I'd just discovered that I had feet, searching for something feasible to say, before mumbling a feeble, "I don't know."

But, when she asked you, you paused for a moment. It was like you were considering the most sensible responses, but in the end, you'd decided that only the truth was suitable. You said, "I just want to be alive." Remember that?

Moms pulled us in for a tight Mama-Bear hug and squeezed us with a mix of heartache and hope. Her sad eyes brimmed with the salty tears of condolence for our improbable futures.

'...And who'd think in elementary, Hey! I'd see the penitentiary one day...' Pac wasn't playin' when he spit that!

I spent twenty-two years confined and confused behind those same grim-gray walls that you stare at every day. There were times when I felt like I was mired in quicksand, stuck in a perpetual doggy-paddle, fighting to keep my head above the muck. There were moments when I didn't even care if the sun showed up for work the next morning. I was physically, emotionally, and psychologically empty. But I couldn't give up. I wouldn't. My spirit wanted to be free. The kind of free that we had never known. And you know the sad reality of it all is: I'd placed far more restrictions on myself, than prison ever had.

You know, yesterday I enjoyed a nice walk with my wife. Oh yeah, I didn't tell you, huh? I'm married now! Can you believe it?! I'm in love, and in love with being in love! HAHAHA! And I mean that soft, poetic, "...raindrops on roses, and whiskers on kittens" kinda love!

My wife's name is Mirra. She's Ghanaian, gorgeous, and the center of my soul-er system. I now understand why men put empires at risk and will gamble away their power, all for the object of their affection. Crazy ain't it? Anyway, I'll print out some photos and send them in the next letter.

So, yesterday we walked through Paris, doing all the "touristy" stuff, seeing the historical landmarks, the museums, and enjoying the French cuisine. But I was struck by how polite and affable the French people are. I mean, a few people looked at me like I was a pork-chop in Pakistan, but the majority of the Parisians are nice. Their smiles seem genuine. You know?

I explained to Mirra that in my neighborhood growing up, we didn't see very many smiles. Our elders, some of whom may have known us since conception, didn't even speak to us without curse words or threats. Not that I can blame 'em, right? Most of our days were wasted away either dodging the police or raising some kind of unnecessary ruckus.

But even if we weren't in the 'hood, if we'd gone far away, out of the inner-city, where nobody knew us, people still treated us like we were less than worthy of common respect. Were we? I mean, you get what you give, right?

It's bonkers, but their loathsome disregard some-how validated our want for ill-repute. Women would clutch their purses tighter, and men crossed the street to avoid having to walk past us. Again, can't say I blame 'em.

Mirra asked me why we wanted infamy? What is its

value? What had created such a void in our young lives that we had to fill it with such violence and villainy?

I didn't have an answer.

She asked me, what were the conditions of our lives that had convinced us that pain doesn't hurt? That love isn't to be shared, instead to be kept and protected for fear that it'll be taken away?

Still, I didn't have an answer.

So, as I was saying, we strolled through Paris, along the River Seine, then picnic'd beneath the sun in the park. (Told' ja I was in love, didn't I?) We then walked to the Arc D'Triomphe, a monument that was erected and dedicated to their beloved emperor, Napoleon Bonaparte. They built this gigantic memorial for this dude, just to say, "Thank You. We recognize your duty and service."

Wow, I thought. Where is our monument?! We've given our childhoods and adulthoods, pledged our loyalties and made commitments to our backstreet brigades and terror squads! We don't get a trophy or ribbon or anything? We retire honorably after surviving the beatings and stabbings and shootings and betrayals and ambushes and life sentences, and, we get.. Nothing? No severance package? No golden parachute? NOTHING?! There's no 401k for gangstas...

Damn!

And the irony of our honorable service to the dishonorable cause is, even after we've given our all to the gang and the gangsterism, to the 'hood and the homeboys, we still can't just quit. NO! Now the same comrades that we rose up and fell down with, want to beat you, stab you, or shoot you for outgrowing the "pack mentality", and choosing to be an individual. Because you yearn for independence. Because you want better for yourself.

Damn!

Imagine if, say, Colin Powell, had announced his retirement after decades of meritorious service to the armed forces, only to have five of his homeboys, some of whom he'd actually trained, jump him, beat him unconscious, and then stab him. "Now you can retire!" they'd tell him.

Last night after our walk, Mirra and I took in the nightlife. We went to a pub in an area populated mostly by North Africans, where I met a man from Morocco named Musa. We began talking about America, its paradoxical glamorization of its own urban underdevelopment, and how Hollywood exploits it all. While I was talking, explaining my own opinions about the subject, Musa noticed my tattoos and asked about them. I explained somewhat boastfully that they were my gang tattoos, my "tribal markings", and that they were used to identify myself to foes and allies alike.

"Our tattoos", I said, "are displayed with pride, and are sometimes indicative of our valor and fidelity to our tribes."

Musa spit water all over himself trying in vain to contain his laughter. Once he'd regained his composure, he promptly dissected my proud and arrogant proclamation, broadcasting for all within earshot, the inconsistencies of my synthetic philosophy,

Musa said we stood for nothing, fought for nothing, and therefore, died for nothing. We achieved nothing!

No rights. No property. No liberation.

    Homie, I was peeved and impressed at the same time! Musa, with his thick, musical accent, and long, swaying, brown-gray dreadlocks, had taken my pride and ego, chopped them up, grilled 'em, and fed 'em to me. Humility had never been served up more tastefully.

    When Mirra and I returned home it was nearly midnight. We made love, punctuating the close of another awesome day, then I held her close to me until she dozed off. For a moment I listened to the lullaby that was her light breathing. The gentle lilt of my sleeping beauty helped calm the chaos that had just previously been my inner peace. The weight of Musa's words, the audacious truth of it all, had stirred me unexpectedly.

    Quietly, I removed myself and went out on our veranda. I stood beneath the ochre ambiance of the full Parisian moon, and I cried. I cried until I was dehydrated, homeboy, but it was the best cry I'd ever had.

    And that's what made me think about writing you this letter. We've invested SO much of our time and energy and lives into... What? I mean, imagine if we invested that same time and effort into being, I don't know, educated. Who knows where we'd be right now. Imagine if we wanted more for ourselves and worked harder at having more, instead of working hard for, well, nothing. Imagine even, if we worked together, as a unit, as a machine, so that we'd all have more. Our families, Our neighbors, Our communities. If it can be thought about, it can be brought about, right?

    Anyway, I hadn't expected to write this much. I'd actually planned to send you a postcard! HAHAHA!

But I miss you, homie. We've been friends since the third grade, and now we're flirting with our forties! DAMN! HAHAHA!

Well, Mirra will be home in a bit, and I gotta get dinner started. It's my night to burn, and there's nothin' like a good ol' greasy American bacon-cheeseburger with a side of curly fries!

Before I go, let me say this. You can't find what you're looking for, until you know what you want. You can't be who you're supposed to be, until you know who you are. Can you dig it?

Give as you'd like to receive, homie. Moms taught us that. If we'd all just treat each other as we ourselves would like to be treated, there'd be no place for jealousy, greed, or envy. Moms taught us that too.

I love you, homeboy. Be safe, be smart, and cross that finish line.

Always, Forever, and Beyond...

Me.

March 2012

Girl On The #7 Bus

Her smile a patchwork pattern of giddiness and glee, eyes that could narrate a silent movie, sista's tone was the hue of Frappuccino creme, hairs the length span of a gnat's breath... she's so anti-social, no Instagram, no facebook, just her notepad, her over-worked pencil, lead dull to the quick, scribblin' mad thoughts, lyric by lyric...a poet she answered, the gleam in her iris glistened a challenge. i deferred...i just wanted to time-share her breathin' space, no covid concerns, her mask was an inviting smile, broken-heart mendable kissable lips, i was just trying not to stutter.....a raised eyebrow criticized my reply, she'd offered to lift my spirits with the essence of herbal blessing. i declined.....i used to, i'd said, put on Jay's Reasonable Doubt, inhale, and just... write. ...Italy, Mykonos, West Indies, Ethiopia, i'd visit them all the day i became rich, i confessed. She leaned in, her eyes clutched my focus, french-kissed my subconscious, you are a bottomless treasure of wordplay of creativity of God-breathed gift of magic and mystery, she said "sweetheart, you're already rich!!" ....Ok, so she didn't say that, but her grin did, when i shared my last effort at poem-whatever-its-called-that-i-write... the #7 bus to haight-ashbury arrived at its next stop, she wished me well, and disappeared, along with the sexy invitation to another confab that i'd wanted to offer.... one last over-the-shoulder glance at me, her pianist's fingers tickled the air goodbye, and she was out of my life forever.... then, I noticed it; she'd left her purse/knapsack on the seat.

I jumped up to call her back, i thought to ask the driver of the #7 to hold up, but she was gone...only the memory of who she would forever be in my heartdrive remained...i snatched her bag, held it, as if to protect it, clutched it to cherish it, vowed to see her again to return it...the hole in its bottom was rival'd only by its designed opening, and it held nothing...potential? promise? hope?...isn't that what life (love) is?

what's in your knapsack....?

October 4th, 2020

Writer's Insight

This was my first bus ride - first *city* bus ride that I had taken since I was a teen.
I was wide-eyed and excited.
The world was still under Covid conditions, so faces were obscured by N95's and surgical masks.
Except for those of us Defiant Ones.
Then she stepped aboard the bus...defiant, attractive, free.
The Girl On The #7
Driving down Market Street,
In San Francisco…

A Convo About Crutches

HIM: Man, I never realized how much I depended on her - she's my rock, my comforter, my friend. She supports me through it all; thick, thin; good, bad, and ugly.

ME: So, she's your crutch?

HIM: Yeah. I lean on her when I can't stand on my own two. Ya know?

ME: Do you appreciate her, bro?

HIM: Hell Yeah! She-

ME: Do you tell her that you appreciate her?

HIM: Yep. All the time.

ME: Do you show her?

HIM: Yep.

ME: Ok...I'm just asking, 'cause the funny thing about "crutches" is that they tend to get tossed in the corner of the closet when they're no longer useful.

HIM: (pause) I'm not really followin' you, big bro. I don't understand what you're saying.

ME: Well, the person who uses a crutch to get by - usually when that person is disabled, or crippled - relies so heavily on the crutch, that he becomes totally dependent on it, like it's an adequate replacement for his natural abilities as an able-bodied man. However, as time goes on, the person becomes well, regains independence, and then tosses the trusted crutch to the corner to become a coat rack.

In other words, li'l bro, don't ever forget the women - mom, granny, sisters, girlfriends - who stood by you, who bore your

burdens right along with you, who you leaned so heavily on. Don't get free and fully functional, then just shove those ladies aside…
HIM: *I got you, big bro.*
ME: *…'Cause in this style of life, you never know when you' gon' stumble into a dys-abling situation and need that crutch to lean on again.*
HIM: *Thank you, B.*

7 Sept. '19

Writer's Insight

This conversation took place outside of the door to the cell that I was assigned to in California
Medical Facility, in Vacaville, California.

I was, among other things, a mentor to the young prisoners. As a former gang banger, I had alot to share for anyone who was looking for success on a pro-social spectrum after repeated failure on an anti-social one became redundant.

One younger brotha that I had often offered direction to had come to me on a weekend afternoon after a visit with his grandmother. He was elated about the visit, but then began to speak about a young woman that he had been communicating with romantically…

A conversation about crutches is what we talked about.

I Wonder…

I wonder…Does Light ever desire to be Dark?
Does Cold envy Warmth? Is jealousy the idolatrous lust of Wet when it contemplates Dry?
I wonder, is covetousness a human heart condition? Is it natural and logical to want something that is so far beyond one's grasp that it's virtually - essentially - a violation of every law of logic and nature?

Does the Leopard envy the stripes of the Tiger?
The mane of the Lion?
The alacrity of the Cheetah?

Is it possible that the youngest Sprout, the most tender Blade of grass, has aspirations to exceed the majesty of the elder Elm Tree?

I wonder, is it ridiculous for the once Wicked to strive for redemption?
Does Evil ever want for Love…for Affection…for Comfort and Consolation?
Is that illogical?
Does Good ever flirt with Bad?
If so…Why?
What could possibly seduce Beauty to span the spectrum for a taste of Hideous?
Curiosity? Audacity?

If Love is capable of Wrath...is it conceivable that the Nefarious could crave Joy?

I wonder...Does the devil also smile?

Written May 2019

#BeautifullyTorn

Me: *What's good, sis?*
Her: **Ironic…I just asked myself the same thing…I feel like I'm being pulled in 2 (too) different directions: my heart can't understand the brain's obsession with logic; my brain can't comprehend the heart's philosophy on emotion…**
Me: *Ironic…I've never seen you more beautiful.*
Her: **Beautifully torn…**
She told me that her heart screams for revenge, blood-thirsty, brutally cold…like just-ice.
Her: **…But, it's my rationale that's tellin' me I'm being irrational…How can I cry 4 the murdered, yet cry 4 murder? "That which I hate, I do…"**
Me: *The book of Romans, chapter 7, verse 15…Amen.*
A solitary tear, melancholy in its descent, meandered against her beauty.
Her: **Talking about it doesn't work, thinkin' 'bout it is worse. Destruction devastates and destroys…**
Me: *Then, just love.*

Writer's Insight

There was a sister, a CNA, that worked in the hospital unit that I cleaned and maintained at the California Medical Facility in Vacaville, California. She was a really cool woman that would keep me updated about the things going on in the urban communities.

On one particular day, she came to work and was visibly distraught. It was painfully obvious that she'd been crying. So, I went to her and asked how she was doing. Her young cousin had been murdered. A victim to gang violence, but not apparently gang affiliated.

As a reformed crime-scene instigator, I was tactless. I could only be a shoulder to cry on. She was angry, vengeful, and heartbroken…

So, I poetically recreated our dialogue to create #BeautifullyTorn…

#flashbang!

What if...Gangsters (or, Gangstas) exchanged their weapons of destruction for cameras?
What if, instead of shooting bullets at opponents, they took snapshots?
Instead of the 9mm, they armed themselves with a 35mm...
It would still be a game of "Hide n Seek" or "Cat n Mouse", but in this game, when a foe gets caught slippin', the shots that are taken at him won't leave him without a pulse.
In this game, per the agreed upon terms, when you get caught on film, you're outta commission for a week. After the duration of those seven days, you can resume play.
Instead of the "rat-tat-tat-tat" of a fully-auto Kalishnikov, it will be the "clik-clik-clik-clik" of a fully-auto Nikon with the extended tripod!
I mean, what if…?

Writer's Insight

As silly as it may seem, I still think about the "what if" alternatives to street gang violence.

As someone who once fervently promoted on-sight destruction of my rivals, I now look back and wish that I had more influence on the youth and the fools who are still pursuing self-destruction in place of self-realization.

Myriad alternatives, yet cannibalism is mode du jour...

#Isolated Chaos

Senate Bill 1077, infamously referred to as - "Isolated Chaos" - is the Bi-Partisan remedy for America's gang and crime epidemic, it's ever-increasing prison population, and, it's answer to the influx of "Deplorable Denizens", who scuttle through every crevice and crack in her vulnerable borders.
This plan, as outlined by the zealous pomposity that is POTUS du jour, is to empty the state of Georgia of its law-abiding citizens, move them all to much better housing throughout the remaining 49 contiguous states, and reimburse all who relocate with "great paying employment and living opportunities."
In return for the eviction, the state of Georgia will then be populated with every criminal, every gang member, and every prisoner in America. *Every,* as in *all.*
The President's reasoning behind such an absurd plan is actually rather simple.
"If these people can't adhere to society's laws, and are constantly jeopardizing the safety and sanctity of the average taxpayer," the Commander-In-Chief spewed, "Let's put 'em all on an island and let 'em kill each other!"
That "island" soon became the Peach State, and before anyone could figure if the Prez was serious, the Bill was passed and signed into action.
After two years of financial configuring, the ten million-plus people that fit the criteria were shipped out, and the four million-or-so candidates - all deplorable in one sense

or another - were shipped in. The people of "New Georgia Republic" were each injected with a microchip that not only tracked them to within a nano-inch of accuracy, it also carried a lethal charge that could be activated if anyone attempted to abscond beyond state lines in any direction.

As predicted, the ensuing settling-in was bloody and despicable.

Until it all changed…

sometime/someday/2018

Writer's Insight

Originally this idea was about an earthquake that shook Los Angeles loose from its state to become an island in the Pacific. The law-abiding survivors would be replaced with the prisoners, parolees, gangsters and wretched dregs of society…
And it was imagined as a video game.
Imagine that…

Look, Just Listen…
(A Love Letter)

What sense does it make for a woman, who is perfectly fit, perfectly healthy, to go to her doctor, and request that she be surgically operated on to find something wrong with her?
It doesn't.
Likewise, what sense does it make for a man whose car runs smoothly, purrs nicely, functions properly, to go to a mechanic and plead that his automobile be opened up, dismantled, and dissected, to find a reason for it to malfunction?
It would be insane, right?
If something is already running better than anyone could expect, or hope for, why would one search for something to be amiss…?

I know that a lot of times, we as rational, reasonable human beings, do things that can be perceived as irrational, unreasonable, and outright dysfunctional. Sometimes we are merely operating on routine; sometimes, it's purely habit. Our experiences often tailor our perceptions, our expectations, and our attitudes.
Simply put: we been thru some shit.
From a personal perspective, I am dangerously in love with the woman of my dreams. I have never known a love that is both passionate and romantic, that is exciting yet fulfilling;

and that is utterly the completion and initiation of my forward momentum.
I wouldn't change anything about this woman except her last name…and in time, I will do just that.
But…
I would just like for this woman, MY woman, to trust me, to see with her third eye, that she doesn't have to dig and scratch and prod into the flesh of our unified body to find something that doesn't exist.
The past has passed, my love.
Your past, my past, both, have been left behind us. Ghosts of what was still haunt us, but they can never hurt us.
Only we can.
Cheaters cheat. Haters hate. But lovers love…and, true love conquers all.

I love u. I am in love with u. Nothing and nobody can compare to u. I want u and ONLY u.
I would never treat u like someone who has hurt me in the past, I would never hold u accountable for something someone else has done to me.
NEVER
Similarly, I shouldn't be seen as an equal to someone that u despise. If ur ex has hurt u, caused u to distrust men, made u get outta character, has disrespected u…I'm sorry.
But I'm not him.
I respect u as a female, as a mother, and as the only woman who I will give my last name to.
And I would NEVER forfeit what we have and what we are building, for something or someone who is not worthy to tie ur shoes.

PERIOD
So…
Please, ladies, try to find it inside of u to walk by faith, not by sight, sound, or fears. Trust in ME, not in men.
I don't want to be with anyone but u. And if there comes a day that there is no more u, or no more us, then, and ONLY then, will I consider being with someone else.
My word…
B

The Juggler

Yesterday, I saw a man at the pier, dressed as a circus clown, face painted into a perpetual frown, juggling three objects: a butcher knife, a chainsaw, and an incomplete Rubik's Cube. He kept it all in constant motion, maintained the proper rotation of each item, and even managed to complete the orange panel on the Cube. I was impressed to say the least. I couldn't help but think about my own juvenile attempt to juggle several delicate objects of affection, staggering beneath the weight of ineptitude and inexperience, nearly folding on a few occasions because I was just simply too naive, or proud, to cry for help. And sadly, much to the surprise of no one, I allowed for one distraction too many, and I dropped every precious item to the floor…it took me nearly 30 years to pick them all up, dust them off, kiss the most precious of them all, and toss aside the broken pieces of the others. Truth is, I didn't begin as a juggler. I was merely a clown; dressing the part, face painted with a perpetual smile, hiding my most intimate sentiments. I was thrust into the spotlight, an emotionally fragile child, convinced by my own imaginings that I could walk the tightrope with no net, blindfolded, and juggle the lives and livelihoods of those closest to me. Again, I never asked for the task, never wanted to be on the big stage. Several times I placed my head in the lions' mouths; I ate fire, chewed glass, and many a night, I laid on a bed of nails. I should've been dead. But I'm still here.

Writer's Insight

Prior to prison, at 16 years old, I was living an adult's life. I was a father, a son, a brother, a friend, a boyfriend, a homeboy, a killer, a fighter, and a giver of too much more than I was willing to offer. I was a juggler.

I juggled life and death and love and hate and indifference and empathy and trauma and insecurity and ego and low self-worth and…

I wasn't very good at it.

So, when I got out of prison, I resisted the pressure to pick up the pieces and toss them all back up in rotation…for a moment. Eventually, I did. And I'm still juggling. Except now, I've dropped some items that will remain where they are.

They were too heavy to begin with…

Who U Talkin' To?

We don't even speak, all we seem to do is bicker with passion
Mumble a couple colorful words, grunt and snort in passin'
How we get here? We were once such an unstoppable force,
Now we're jus' immovable objects, an illogical concept
Is it a lack of trust? Is it insecurity, subtracting "U-S"?
The devil masquerading as an angel of light, distracting us?
All I desired was to belong, to be strong, right or wrong - am I deluded?
The strongest drive in this intangible prison is to feel included
Yet, somehow, we dilute it, our pursuits become perpetual pitfalls
There's no "we" in team, so "I" become the reason that it falls…
In pieces, shattered fragments of Could've and Shoulda been
What woulda been, if we had taken a moment and just been friends…
Take a second, think about who I wrote these words to
The Nation, the races, or to YOU?

Writer's Insight

Republicans vs Democrats…
Blacks vs Whites vs Browns…
Bloods vs Crips…
America vs Everybody…
When does it stop? When did it all begin? Why?
Who am I talking to…?

Truly

I dedicate this to you, my written sentiments, sincerest confessions
I got no hang ups bout my feelings, so I use no discretion
I'll let it flow, let it expose my soul
Allow my potent poetics to paint a proper picture, a portrait of prose
I got a mind fulla notions, hopin', that every word that's spoken
Translates, for my heart's sake, you got me open
Sendin' text messages anticipating your call back
I'm LOL, cauz OMFG, sometimes I fall back
In reverie, daydreamin' vividly bout forever
Together we are forever, baby, believe me i've never
Known a love like yours, so strong, so thorough, I'm sure
That if the world should crumble tomorrow our bond would endure (I love u)
Take my hand, make me a better man, I plan
To be the best that I can be, for us and for we
Its longevity - no doubt - I'm yours til the end
As your husband, your confidant, and your best friend...
Truly

A Necessary Tragedy

Damn, I love her!

Sunny is her name. And like the mighty star, Sunny brings life, and an all-encompassing brilliance to my otherwise frigid world.

I love her so, so much.

I've read that confession is the cleansing of the soul. So, for the purpose of protecting my guilt, and preserving her virtue, I won't speak specifically about the qualities and peculiarities that make Sunny so precious to me. I mean, the fact that she adores all things living and tiny, from kittens to cacti, doesn't take away from the story…

Does it?

'Course not!

From the day that we met, Sunny was a challenge that I couldn't forfeit. The attraction was immediate. After our first exchange, I couldn't get enough. She was the opening passage of a classic novel, and I, the ardent aficionado, was engrossed by her profound magnificence.

I was seven years into a twelve-year prison sentence, chained up for criminal gang activity and unabashed adolescent insanity, when the Sun, somewhat ceremoniously, broke through the sinister-black clouds that had loitered tauntingly above me. I'd been alone, and lonely, for too long. The dread of becoming institutionalized haunted me. I was detached, desensitized, and becoming more beast than being. An emotional and spiritual metamorphosis is what I needed.

Then along came Sunny.

We began as pen-pals, evolved into friendship, then transitioned to the phenomenon of being in love. We wrote every day, and when I was paroled five years later, it was the sweetest meeting of two hearts since Tristan and Isolde. Our passion knew no bounds; our adventures had no limit. For the first time ever, I was in love. My once slate-gray skies were now a pristine blue. In the center, high above, was my bright, wonder-full source of the purest joy.

That is, until one day, four years after my release from prison - and, from the stranglehold of gang membership, I was waylaid and sucker-punched by an old school enemy named Fate.

Actually, it was more like an unseen, unprovoked and unprepared kick in the nuts.

Yep, *just* like that.

Sunny had a chronic ailment that much too often affected her kidneys. She'd had fainting spells and minor discomfort in her lower back, long before we'd met. Not a big fan of hospitals and medicinal treatment, she'd often relied on the age-old, time-tested method: ignore it and it'll go away. And that had worked just fine with Sunny. That is, until the day she vomited blood.

The heavens were a horrible shade of Bad-News-Gray when I got the call. I was working at the nursery, unloading a pallet of Azaleas, when Sunny's best friend, Raya, called to tell me that Sunny had fainted again. When she couldn't be revived, the paramedics were called, and Sunny was rushed to the hospital.

To say that I was in a full panic would be akin to saying that a tsunami was no more than a ripple in a rain puddle.

I flew through traffic, blowing past every intersection like I was Steve McQueen on an Epinephrine drip. I fish-tailed into the parking lot at Mercy-General, and sprinted up the stairs, two at a time, to the fifth floor.

The doctors said it was bad. Raya's tears told me it was FUBAR. I burst into Sunny's room and pulled her into my arms. She was pale and fragile, but her arms clutched me, as if our embrace was all the treatment she'd need.

We kissed, we cried, then cried some more.

Only one time before had we cried together…the first time we'd made love. It was magical and explosive, and double rainbows…

But this wasn't.

This was uncompromising pain and anger and denial.

For the next two weeks I lived right there beside Sunny. We ate together, slept together, and every stolen opportunity was spent making her laugh and smile. Only when she napped did I leave her side.

Once, I slipped away to the nursery to get an arrangement of Sunny's favorite flowers; Sun-Bright Marigolds, Pink Lilies, and Electric-Blue Orchids. When I returned, I was met by Sunny's doctor, a pretty, cinnamon-colored woman, with a thick Mid-Eastern accent. She pulled me aside and began explaining succinctly how powerless and ineffectual my hopes and wishes were. She sprinkled in something about insurance and a lack of bed space, and how Sunny's nationality could hinder finding a donor-match for transplant. Sunny needed a full replacement of both kidneys, and being of mixed heritage meant it would be harder finding compatibility.

Dr. Cinnamon also said that our hope solely rested on finding someone of Sunny's paternal lineage. It might increase our odds. But, without insurance, or a miracle, hope was all we had.

I kissed her parched lips and handed Sunny her flowers. She sniffed deeply their fragrant reward, then set them aside. I pulled back the covers, climbed in beside her, and held Sunny close. I stroked her hair gently, wiped away a stray tear, and *kisspered* tender reassurances in her ear.

I had to find a solution…somehow.

Ten minutes' drive from the city that we called ours, lies a small immigrant community that Sunny often visited. She'd say that it reminded her of her late father, the culture, the food, its nostalgic ambiance.

It was there that I would find Sunny's donor.

Except, I wasn't planning to negotiate or persuade someone to donate.

I would make that decision for them.

The malignant miscreant that I had been prior to meeting Sunny was always just a scratch beneath the veneer. Not that I had been artificial with her, but honestly, I had been a fighter far longer than I'd been a lover.

I was fostered in the open wound of urban underdevelopment. And like gravel in that open wound, I painfully infected, and grossly stunted the growth of, my community. As an adamant activist for juvenile revolt, I subscribed to the street maxim: fight for what you need, take what you want, and, by all necessary means, protect what you have.

Sunny had rescued me from that anti-lifestyle. She had made me human. My bull-in-a-China Shop-like re-entry into society was a test of our emotional fortitude and patience.

Together we persevered. Sunny introduced me to unconditional love and unfaltering passion for life.

I couldn't lose my Sunny.

I combed that tiny community, each residential thoroughfare, stalking every potential target. I had decided to aim for the "Green and Clean" crowd. The young, carefree, college-aged adults seemed more likely to be organ donors.

A random, cold-blooded murder wasn't beneath me. Not when the prize was a body with fresh, healthy organs, that could possibly save Sunny's life.

I drove into a shopping mall parking lot and parked. The damp Wednesday night was a bit warm considering the season, but not unusual. I settled in and waited.

It wasn't long before the first pigeon appeared. She was spry, sporty, and walking alone, bobbing her head to the music playing from her earbuds, unaware.

I opened the car door and set my foot out. The thick, cool air hit me like a splash of water, bathing me with an unsettling sense of purity.

As she speed-walked along, I calculated the distance between us. Running stealthily, minding my shadow, I could easily creep up and ruin her life.

I considered it.

Watching…

Contemplating…

My heart beat a rumba rhythm in my throat.

The pocket-sized .25 caliber pistol rested discreetly in my palm. I clicked off the safety and fingered the curve of its trigger…

Then, I stepped back into the car.

She very likely was somebody's Sunny.

I drove to another area, another neighborhood, feeling more melancholy than before, but still so very determined.

The niggling taunt of morality reverberated in the lightless attic that was my brain.

I should stop this. It's wrong, and-

NO! Right there! Walking down a solemn side-street, *ALONE*, probably heading home from work or possibly going to a girlfriend's house, was my mark. Trudging along, head bowed, face illuminated by his cellphone.

Oblivious…

Slowly, I drove past him. He never looked up to see the stranger in the ominous sedan, tailing him, prowling like Simba in the tall desert grass. I drove on, turned the first corner, and threw the car in park. Leaving the engine running, I hopped out. Whether hold-up or homicide, the getaway was crucial.

I headed toward my victim. The mini semi-automatic felt warm in my pasty grip. I pocketed my hands and marched onward.

"Excuse me", I said, as I shoulder-checked him in passing.

I hadn't noticed at first, but he was wearing glasses. Perplexed, he acknowledged my apology with a slight nod but said nothing.

He kept walking.

I spun effortlessly, pushed my pistol behind his right ear, and squeezed the trigger.

* * *

Unapologetically selfish, I may be. But who among the living wouldn't secure their love, the fount of their happiness, by all possible means?

I mean truly, isn't my own happiness more important to me than anyone else's?

Yet, despite my nefarious efforts, my beautiful, bright Sun fell deep below the horizon, beyond any hope for return.

The boy, Christian, his name was, indeed had been an organ donor, and, amazingly, was a perfect match for Sunny.

But he had also matched perfectly for Arabella.

Arabella was nine years old, and I swear, if God created anything more precious than her, He kept it for Himself.

She'd been a patient in the hospital for more than a year, and she topped the donor list.

It's been a year since Sunny died. One year ago, today.

And she donated her organs.

The End.

> ### Writer's Insight
> This is my first story ever completed and typed out. It's the introduction to my heart and my mind, and to my soul as a writer. My attempt at producing a "Tragedy", my first confession of a compassionate felon.

The Dark Side of Truth

"…And, as time continues to move forward, the world grows more weary…", his voice boomed authoritative and sprightly, reaching the ears of those whose approval he sought, "…Mankind practices evil continually."

Xander Truman, effervescent and academically adroit, spoke into the microphone, addressing the United States Senate Committee about his solution to what has been the ever-increasing crime rate. At thirty-eight years old, Xander had become the fastest rising senator America had ever seen. His boyish good looks and capricious charm belied his off-the-chart I.Q. and Protestant wisdom.

"In fact, ladies and gentlemen, even the Bible tells of the decline of society as the end draws near. Now for those of you who are of different faiths and religions, or for those who simply do not believe in anything, your hearts - your blue-blooded souls - may attribute a rise in crime and unrighteousness to everything from global warming to gluten." He grinned, flashing dimples that could melt butter.

"But for me, it's as plain as sugar is sweet. In the Bible, in 2 Timothy, chapter 3, the Word of God says, and I'm paraphrasing, '…that men will be lovers of themselves…' Wow! Ladies and gentlemen of the Senate, if I were to stop there…"

The captive audience of political fuddyduds and stalwart statesmen all chuckled earnestly, Xander's jest allowing for a glimmer of levity.

"Ok, ok. So, God said that men will be lovers of themselves, lovers of money, proud, unloving, unforgiving, brutal, lovers of pleasure rather than lovers of God...traitors, despisers of good…. Need I go on?"

The rhetorical question hung heavy in the silence.

Xander Truman was not only a rising star in the political stratum, but he was also a devout servant of his Lord and Savior, Jesus Christ.

Born and bred in the backwater township of Wibaux County, Montana, Xander led a spotless life of home-schooling, Biblical scrutiny, and moral essentiality, all honed under the prudent discipline of his mother, Cressida, who had been widowed only four months into her pregnancy with Xander; and his Great-Aunt, Miss Jessamina, a tried-and-true tomboy without replicate.

After serving his country as an Air Force Reserve, Xander attended Harvard Law School, then Yale, before entering politics full time.

It was while serving as an intern, his first year in D.C., that he and his friends designed and manufactured what they believed would radically improve law enforcement and make the great states of America secure again.

"My fellow Americans, as the Word of God warns, times will continue to increase in peril and repugnance as the depravity of mankind spirals deeper and faster down the drain. Those who commit their wicked acts in the dark are living in fear of the light."

Xander pulls from his suitcoat pocket a tiny device - no bigger than a breath mint - and sits it on the edge of the table before him.

Several people lean forward, adjusting their glasses trying to see the miniscule gadget.

"Two years ago, my colleagues and I designed this little gismo that we've named, 'The Light of Truth' settles just beyond the inner nostril, in the crevice of the cranial pocket, emitting a color-coded glow that can be seen by all, everywhere. It cannot be obscured or concealed in any way. It will never burn out or need to be replaced. And it's completely harmless to its carrier."

A faint murmur wafted among the congressmen and women.

"Uh, Mister Truman, what exactly is it that you're proposing with this, uh, nasal…thing?" Asked the stodgy elder statesman, Rutherford Cranston.

"Thank you for asking, sir. Allow me, if you will, ladies and gentlemen, to clarify for you exactly how 'The Light of Truth' will not only lower the crime rate but will ultimately put an end to the *multi-billions* that America hemorrhages annually with the National Prison Industrial Complex."

Again, murmurs rose to an audible din as the audacious projection swept the large conference room.

"Imagine, if you will, someone commits a crime, say, an armed robbery. They're caught, charged, tried and convicted. Yet, instead of a prison cell, they're implanted with 'The Light of Truth', which, for the crime of robbery, emits a bright green light from the bridge of their nose up to the hairline of the forehead.

"As a convicted criminal they will forever be identified by their light. No longer will they be able to creep nefariously on the unsuspecting to commit their despicable crimes. No longer can they blend in with society under the guise of law-abiding citizens, biding their time, plotting and scheming more and more acts of lawlessness.

Each crime is designated by a distinct color: Red is for murder; Green, as I've said, is for robbery, theft, larceny; Purple is for rape; Orange for pedophilia; and so on. Our tax-paying, hard-working, iron-blooded American citizens will no longer be duped by the clever con artist or the malignant murderer."

Every eye focused - unblinking - on Xander Truman.

If his inspiring spiel had the esteemed members of the United States Congress considering his proposal, it was the finish that sold them completely.

"My fellow patriots, countrymen and women, our lives - our very *history* - is sewn in the quilted fabric of freedom and diversity; those same attributes that are constantly being threatened.

"When we put an end to the cancerous crimes that plague our beloved nation with 'The Light of Truth', imagine how we can change the world! Terrorists, convicted of conspiring against America and our allies, will forever be identified by 'The Light of Truth'! We'd see 'em comin' - and hidin' - from miles away! Amen?

"God Bless America!"

* * *

The following year, Xander Truman's proposal to congress was set in motion. "The Light of Truth" passed overwhelmingly without opposition.

Xander suddenly became the golden boy of the senate.

Swiftly, yet efficiently, the climate of violence changes across the states, including an eradication of violent or perverse television programming, movies, music and published literature.

Within five years, America becomes ultra-vanilla.

The "Detestables", or, "Dt's", as they have come to be known, take to the underground, existing in colony-like subsections of the larger metropolitan communities. The separation from "The De-Lighted" society creates a discriminatory class system based on arrogance and prejudice, as opposed to financial stability or ethnicity, which fosters a smoldering animosity.

However, the emergence of a team of uber-hackers, a duo, known only as, "N. Sidious" and "Ann R. Kee", bring everything to a jarring halt. When it's discovered that the villainous technological savants are disabling the implants, the dormant beast that is every kind of evil is suddenly awakened.

And Xander Truman is the object of its appetite.

A Fotograf 2020

Ive been fixed here for 28 years
Likened 2 a faded, framed artifact
A relic of nostalgia
A "living", breathing, thinking fotograf
I evoke memories of colorful yesterdays,
Provoke audacious hope of mornings after…
Yet, as surely as the eye blinks
I evaporate from thought…

19 March 20

What I See in The Tenderloin

Life gets in a retina, like jagged shards of silica...bombarding my senses with real-time exclamations (!!!!!!!) of dog crap on graffiti scarred sidewalks....minglings of yesterday's desires, youthful imaginings, now decrepit and sick, beauty never quite fades - it takes on shades of hideousness.... steaming piles of neverwas regrets, hefty-bagged, sitting like defeated Sumo rejects...brand-newness juts out from completed reconstruction, a pregnant belly, amidst the forsaken facades of financial idolatry....bodies, barely breathing, litter sidewalks, a smorgasmorgue of detritus and deferred dreams...irony slaps my awed face, clips my jaw ajar, surprise is the insecure sister to shock....an envious shade of Crayola rolls by with gleaming rims, limo-tint windows, Nipsey haunting the airwaves....such a paradox to contemplate...."NO HUMAN BEING IS ILLEGAL" muralized on the wall...it's the tenderloin district…

September 23, 2020

Writer's Insight

It's the Tenderloin District.
"Nuff said.

The Peoples' Liaison (Just An Idea)

SUMMARY

Note: At the time of this writing, I was still in prison. I had been recently denied parole by a Governor's Reversal, after a finding of suitability by the BPH in 2019.

My name is Brian Shepperd, I am 45 years old, and I have been in prison for 29 years, since I was 16 years old.

Throughout the majority of my time, particularly within the last decade, I have listened to many conversations between lifers concerning the parole board hearing process, and how biased and unbalanced it is. Gripes and grievances from prisoners should not come as a surprise to anyone, considering the disproportionate statistics of parole grants versus denials, historically speaking, of course. Within the past few years things have become progressively better in regard to findings of suitability, but for some there is still the Governor's review that presents an equally daunting obstacle to overcome.

January 16, 2019, I went before the parole board for my subsequent suitability hearing. After six hours of questions and answers I was found suitable for release back into society. Being told by the Commissioner that I am no longer deemed a threat to society was the most validating sensation that I will probably ever experience. However, after the four-month review by the Parole Committee, the Governor was given his lawful opportunity to sign off on my release, or to reverse the Parole Board's decision. He decided that the latter was the better option, citing in his judgement that, "Mr. Shepperd('s)... rehabilitation is still in progress and requires further development before he can be safely released."

Also, the achievements and/or accolades that our Governor acknowledged in my favor were relegated to three sentences within the entire report: "I also acknowledge that Mr. Shepperd has made some efforts to improve himself in prison. He earned his G.E.D. and has been employed. He also engaged in programming."

Such vague concessions in such a limited space offer nothing in the way of a balanced and fair summarization of my nearly three decades in prison, most of which were while being housed in maximum-security prisons. It certainly says nothing about my day-to-day programming of the last decade.

For a lot of lifers, specifically, those of us with a murder conviction, the Governor's review is the highest hurdle.

In fairness, the Governor's decision is based on his understanding of the transcripted record from the parole hearing, and not necessarily from a review of an inmate's actual Central File (C-File) or psychological evaluation report. If an inmate fails to speak about his/her personal accomplishments, academic achievements, or pro-social activities, then the Governor has only what is within his reach to render his verdict.

It is my humble opinion that society deserves the assurance of its governing body to examine thoroughly, exhausting every available remedy, to fairly approve or deny it's rehabilitated citizens as we return to our respective communities

PROPOSAL

This proposal is an effort to ensure fairness for all who are involved in parole suitability hearings, to provide a well-rounded process for effective decision making.

The average prisoner who is taking his/her rehabilitation seriously is more often than not enrolled in several self-help programs, is employed full-time, and has accumulated a dossier of certificates and laudatory chronos. Although an inmate such as this may be an example of positive programming, it doesn't guarantee that he/she will be found suitable for parole.

Similarly, the same kind of prisoner could go before the Parole Board and provide adequate insight, express heartfelt remorse, and accept responsibility for his/her crimes; recite the 12-Steps of sobriety, articulate every anti-crime/anti-violence mantra, and have a city's population-worth of support letters. Again, it doesn't ensure that he/she is being sincere and non-manipulative before the deciders of his/her fate.

A People's Liaison would bridge the gap between what is said by the inmate and what can be substantiated by those who interact with him/her regularly, e.g., housing unit officers, work supervisors, program facilitators, et al, providing for more informed decision making. The Liaison's interview with such people would be random, yet specific, to confirm or disqualify any claims made by the inmate.

As well, the Liaison could be afforded an opportunity to attend an open session of a self-help group, offering insight to the participants into what qualities a representative for the people is looking for as an interviewer; and he or she could relate officially what strides are actually being made on the proactive and pro-social front.

In conclusion, it is my opinion, based on my own experience with parole hearings and having had my suitability reversed, that providing more clarity and data-gathering allows for the Governor's decision making to be based on confirmed information that corroborates the transcripted record. A Liaison that operates on behalf of the People would be neither pro-inmate, nor pro-BPH. Instead, its findings would be pro-society, providing balance for all parties involved.

3hree After 3hirty

30/3...
...I work in the service of the less fortunate, the unhoused, the emotionally and mentally unstable, the substance abusers; I'm making living amends for the cosmic thievery that I've committed for almost 5 decades, while helping to make significant changes in people's lives....and, still, I struggle with feelings of guilt, shame, and being unforgivable. There are times when my best efforts to be positive and forward thinking become distorted transmissions, as if my spirit has poor wifi...

30/3...
...I have real friends. Not homies or associates or affiliates, but real friends. It's a feeling of completion in some sense. As a kid I had friends and we shared EVERYTHING! Friendship was special, it was sacred, and it was designed to be eternal. In alot of ways it was...My friendships now are much more genuine. The range of emotional depth is matured, and there's really no space for superficiality. As a youth, our bond was centered in shared pain. Now, our unified energy is focused on healing...

30/3...
...my mom is my everything! I mean, she trained me to fight fair, and how to fight dirty. She learned me on the art of being sly, slick and wicked, and the etiquette to be a

gentleman. Moms kept me properly prepared preventing poor performance, yet she showed me that improvisation and adaptability are powerful tools...this morning, 9/11/23, my most cherished human being passed away. 82 years old. A mighty spirit that will forever accompany me along the way. I love you, Ma...

Suffocation

2 lungs fulla night air, chase away the nightmares...
I close my eyes and suddenly I'm back right there..
Who said that demons had to fight fair..?
Au contraire, post-traumatic stress strangles every breath...
despair.

In No Sense

If I was voiceless, how could I tell you that I was innocent of your cruel accusations?
Could I demonstrate a character that everso obviously counters the very allegations that you level against me...?

If I were blind, in which way would you show me that you come in peace, that you haven't the faintest intentions of causing me harm?
Would you speak in humble tones that truly belie the sinister misconceptions to persuade my otherwise caustic cynicism therefore to receive your offered hand?
And, if I reciprocated, would you only believe my intentions were harmless because of my (dys)ability?

If I lacked the sensation of touch, to feel, would you pity me or patsy me?
Would you teach me why heat is hot? Why cold is death? Why LOVE is comforting and protective?

Our common sense is to falsely assume that all of our senses are common...LOVE burns as hot as HATE.
DEATH is as cold as IGNORANCE.
PAIN translates as vividly as COMPASSION...
...even if BLIND hate is SENSELESS.

Jus' Cauz

Just cauz I can't PROVE my innocence, don't mean I am guilty...
In the United Snakes of Los Angeles, Just Cause aint the same as Justice... just is...

Just 'cauz your deepest, ugliest, most horrible secrets aren't readily available for social dissecting...duzn't mean that you could/would/should excavate my skeletons to autopsy my history...
DO UNTO OTHERS AS YOU WOULD HAVE THEM DO UNTO YOU

Just 'cauz you peer from the dark recesses of your tinted glass house windows, pointing fingers like sniper rifles, chunkin' boulders and stones at the scenes of the before-my-eyes-life as they flash like social media gifs...duznt mean that the simplest pebble can't/won't ricochet and shatter the facade of your not-so-crystal-cathedral that you hide falsely secure behind…

Less Than Zero

U Cut me, I scream
U stab me, I bleed
Pointed fingers (like 9 millimeters)
The bringers of judgement & derision,
...Perforates my ambitions..
.....Alternates my decisions..
.......U contemplate my conditions,
.........Then instigate my collision...
"Be a better man"...better than who?(!)
Thirty calendars separate him from me..
...then from now...
...thoughts from beliefs...
...ignorance from understanding...
U Cut me, I cry
U stab me, I plead
Love me, I heal...
We heal.

U Mist Me, Really?

Would you miss me if I left...?
When I left, didju miss me...?
Be honest...
Tangible thoughts are indelible scribblings of sentiments unspoken...
Translation...
U mist me about as long as it took for the vapor to usher the syllables of my name out of your jib, to escape past your lips, into the ether of everything except me, never captured on paper, folded into envelopes, flown to my penitent palms...
Black-and-White photos of withered grass, provoke imaginings of what greener must look like...wilted rose petals still possess their beauty, promoting a pleasant perfume, my personal potpourri...memories was all I had to remind that I was HUMAN, while hope was all I could to encourage my BEING, yet without LOVE I was in-complete & un-equal, i'm-possible, but somehow worth-less...
But U Mist Me..?
Really..?

Auditions

Everyday is really just an audition for a role that you're destined to perform...
You never really know who's presence you're in at any given moment...therefore, you never really know what impression you'll have on someone who very well could put in motion the things that could change your entire trajectory in life…

Butterflies & Hummingbirds

U've given me a joy I'd never dared fathom before
I used to wonder, if I'd disappear, would my memory be mourned..?
My misery adorned my torn sleeve like a liberal's heart
Literal art - tattoo B's answer my soliloquy in part...
Comedy & Tragedy - moods swing like a pendulum
Internal conflict rages, my best efforts are disingenuine
Hesitant, but giving in, I surrendered my fears in forfeit
You pulled away the mask, I tasted pure love from the Source, its...
the warm and fuzzy, it's butterflies & hummingbirds Its the love of words, kissed;
The magic of Black-ness.. The juxtaposition of fantasy & myth...
It's laughing-at-a-funeral funny, it's ironic..
We're a poetic composition set in motion, what we share is iconic...what we are is ionic...

Irony, or Hypocrisy…?

Male figure, mid-20's, collapsed in a rumpled heap, needle plunged near-death-deep into a long-since-collapsed vein…
…his other hand clutches an asthma inhaler…

A pigeon with a limp…
A druggie, smeared face, grime-caked grimace, hair matted and greasy…
…Jordan 11's spotless……

Two men share a meth pipe, use the business end of the same needle…
…Then argue, scratch and fight over a Popeyes drumstick & biscuit ….

Huh?

Fresh outta prison, raw as a Rida's ambition
Icon of contrition - penitence - I conned with condition
Donned a disguise, tried to hide my lies amid visions
Unattainable didn't wanna admit or dismiss it
Truth is…
The me that misses it, is just a hint of a whisper of the me that isn't it
Thought I had what I wanted til I lost what I had
Snatched from my grasp, I clutched and I grabbed
I took and I stole, but I surrendered in the end
Because the me that fought the most, is the me that could never win…

Futile

Sometimes I flirt with the notion of just letting go…
The exhilaration of walking the ledge of the 72nd story,
tempting the imbalance, yet clutching the handrail…
and then letting go.

The fleeting amazement of a red balloon, helium-headed,
bobbing and bouncing with each of my steps, a rare
illustration of moments of levity…then, in a moment's
breath, I loosen my grip on the tether, I let go…

Poof! Be gone…

The whims of insecurity, of resentment, the grudges, the
guilt, the SHAME…
Holding onto long-ago ideas of a King's Ransom and
Scrooge McDuck dives into dunes of gold coins…
Imaginings of a life without worries, without false evidence
appearing real…
It's all juvenile juxtaposition…

It's one of the worst feelings in this thing called life,
Futility…

Milton Keynes UK
Ingram Content Group UK Ltd.
UKHW021343011224
451693UK00009B/728